The Mone

The Money Gym

Ultimate Wealth Workout

Nicola Cairncross

First Published 2005 by Lean Marketing Press

This Edition Published in Great Britain 2010
by Bookshaker.com

I am grateful, not only to my friends and family for putting up with me, but to my entrepreneurial spirit which burns bright and never seems to dim, no matter what challenges and obstacles I have to overcome.

It makes it worth getting up in the morning, every morning, and helps me see life as a great adventure, ensuring I never know what's going to happen next!

Contents

Praise

"Saying Nicola Cairncross helps people with money is like saying that Bill Gates isn't short of a bob or two, or that I wouldn't kick Jennifer Aniston out of bed. Both statements are true, but woefully understated. Nicola doesn't just help people with money, she gets them to start with a blank piece of paper, design their ideal life, then make a plan to get them there. As if that wasn't enough, she helps people do that magical thing of 'being all they can be'"

Peter Stanley, Property Investor and author of Property Made Simple, www.PropertyMadeSimple.com

"I know a few of the people mentioned in The Money Gym book and these are REAL stories of REAL people who have turned a corner and improved their lives by working through the Money Gym process."

Marie Taylor, www.MarieTaylorConsulting.com

"Some fabulous ideas, and very much in tune with not only the global economic climate, but also the way that we (as Money Gym clients) are developing and growing. I feel so grateful to have been introduced to The Money Gym as the benefits of being a part of such a rich and vibrantly resourceful group expand positively into every area of my life. It's so powerful to see how people have used the Money Gym teachings, applied them in their lives and how effective they have been!"

Niki Duffy, www.hypnonik.typepad.com/nikiduffy

"I have to say that if it wasn't for the fact that I came across The Money Gym three years ago, I probably would have had to pack up and go back to working for someone else long ago, because I had no idea what was involved in running a business, and, apart from the ability to type, practically no skills that would help me start up and grow a business. I've learned so much from The Money Gym ... the list goes on and on."

Ann Harrison, www.contemporaryretirementcoaching.com

"I first subscribed to Nicola's e-course (the basis for this book) in 1998, and it totally opened my eyes to just how many options there are for generating income. I've valued Nicola excellent advice ever since. For example, I'm eternally grateful to her for introducing me to the idea of remortgaging my house to generate cash to support the growth of my business. And I love the idea of the Bath of Abundance. Through The Money Gm, Nicola has also created a resourceful, well-informed on-line group, where the advice is powerful (and generous) and the sense of belonging to a community is strong."

Dr Jane P Lewis, www.linesofexperience.com

"I started Nicola's Financial Intelligence Programme which grew into The Money Gym book, when I was renting a flat with 3 friends in North London, had meagre savings that weren't doing very much in a savings account and could never have afforded to buy in London on my £18K per year (salary). I now own 8 UK properties, and part own (with some family members) three properties in France, which are rented out as self catering cottages over the summer months and used off peak as a HQ for extended family get-togethers."

Alice Bagley

"By May 2003 I had discovered Nicola Cairncross and her financial coaching programme called The Money Gym. I was already, at the ripe old age of 47, motoring through my lump sum (from the sale of my accountancy practice) ... I neither owned my own home nor any other property, having had my two homes re-possessed in the horrors following on from the interest rates crisis and knock-on property "crash" at the end of the Eighties ... I had no pension, and no plans for my future. I had no idea how to make money online, was too scared to get back into property, had already sold my business when it reached a critically painful place and was still exchanging time for money, being an accountant part-time for albeit a nice wedge. Nicola changed all that...

1. I have found a way back into owning property, the single most important thing I believe we can do in the UK to improve our wealth. I now own four flats and am on the way to making a portfolio of eleven within the next three years.

2. I know how to make money online, and market my businesses via the internet

3. I was able to give up my 'day job' in February 2007

4. I have been able to learn how to take my twenty five years' business experience and turn it into several Businesses to Love

And yes, in the summer of 2005, Nicola did me the great honour of inviting me to become her business partner and now The Money Gym goes from strength to strength."

Judith Morgan www.JudithMorgan.com

"I'd class myself as a serious businesswoman and entrepreneur and my estimate to date from my involvement with The Money Gym is that my various businesses have benefited to the tune of around £400k without taking into account the ongoing revenue opportunities that I've been putting in place ... One of the main things I've gained is that financial independence can be achieved very quickly, you just need to identify the best route for you and I certainly have done!"

Debbie Bissett, www.DebbieBissett.com

"I am a qualified architect, originally from Scotland and I have lived in London for the last 10 years. At the end of January I was made redundant from a job that I really enjoyed and had worked very hard at for nearly a decade. Property has always been my passion and now I feel I can move forward with the information I am learning and make this passion work for me rather than someone else's company. I can't thank The Money Gym enough for giving clarity to my thoughts and helping me through what I thought at the time was the end of my world. I now realise it was just the start of something really great and being made redundant was the best this that could have happened!"

Martin Young, Scotland

"In 2007 my husband and I had been living in rented property for 12 years with no chance (so I thought) of buying our own place – me being self employed plus having a reasonable amount of debt and no deposit. Thanks both to The Money Gym we moved into our own place on 1st April 2008! We are now firmly on the path to being debt free, I have built and run my own website around one of my passions MotorBikin.com and I have started a video course teaching people how to do their own accounts using simple spreadsheets. I am so glad I found the Money Gym and am looking forward to an exhilarating and wealthy future."

Jakki Francis, www.motorbikin.com

"The Money Gym is for EVERYONE. My journey began so far behind the starter's gun that it has taken a Money Gym year for me to arrive AT the starting line. But here I stand, strong, emotionally secure and confident that I will achieve my goals and so very much richer emotionally, spiritually and materially ... My thinking has moved from that of 'scarcity' to 'abundance'. I know it's all out there waiting for me to collect."

JanetSwift, www.SwiftlySorted.com

"As someone who teaches others how to create great Joint Ventures, I know the value of relationships and of bringing value to other people. In her book, The Money Gym, Nicola definitely over-delivers on the value and shares everything she knows about wealth creation, holding nothing back. Her own passion is internet marketing but the property, business and stock market chapters are just great too and I learned a lot. The parts of the book that deal with the emotional and internal factors that hold us back from creating success – and wealth – for ourselves are covered in a down to earth manner, with lots of great recommendations should you want to pursue that area further. Don't' miss reading The Money Gym, it's destined to be a classic."

Sohail Khan, 7 Figure JV Expert, International Speaker and Author, CEO of the Joint Venture Group and President of The Joint Venture University, www.thejvuniversity.co.uk

Acknowledgements

First of all I would like to acknowledge my mum, who, before she had me, danced on stage in London at the age of 19 in the original production of *The King & I*. She taught me that you can have anything you want if you just want it bad enough and work for it hard enough. Perhaps 'smart enough' might have been less tiring, Mum!

I want to thank my fabulous sisters Heather Cairncross (Altovoice.com) and Sarah Cairncross (Rawrrr.com). Unwavering support for all my mad schemes, lots of humour and straight talking in equal measures.

Then I would like to acknowledge two of my earliest mentors, Dr William Pitt, of Worthing, who was interested in everything and the first grown-up to show an interest in what I thought about things, He bought his first computer in his late 70's and, as well as keeping up with current affairs, spent a lot of time surfing the Xena Warrior Princess website as far as I can tell. He also taught me about fine wine and dining and that, when you pay the bill, you call the shots. Never be intimidated by snooty waiters.

Then the ultimate entrepreneur Bennie Gray of the Space Organisation, who gave me my first 'paradigm shift', by telling me that I was no secretary but management material, who employed me when no-one else would, paid me more than I asked for, gave me the freedom to explore all the principles I was learning from Steven Covey's '7 Habits of Highly Effective People'. He taught me how much more rewarding performance and profit related pay was, and let me go graciously when it was time.

My first life coach, Rachel Turner. How did you cope – I was so remedial on personal development! My second business coach Chris Barrow, who challenged and pushed me to be always better and braver than I thought I was.

Friends – what treasures without price; veterans like my ex-husband Irving Soremekun, stalwart best friend of 35 years Kim Black, Philippa & John Waddell, Marlene & Keith Sanders and newer ones like Guy Levine, Peter Stanley, Tony Gedge and Maria Davies. Not to mention the many wonderful teenager friends of my kids – bringing life to the house and mad fashions wherever they go.

Wealth Mentors, first of which was Gill Fielding, who changed my thinking totally, taught me about and daily demonstrated so well, about living by the principles of the Sea of Abundance and many of the other concepts in this book. Andy & Greg, who taught me how to think totally differently about property.

And last, but by no means least, my wonderful friends and business partners. First up, Steve Watson. You resisted all this coaching stuff for years, didn't you, but it's sinking in slowly and accidentally. You are an amazing person, a great graphic designer and for years a great stand-in dad to Phoebe & Nelson who love you loads. I hope that we have only just begun our wealth creation journey!

Judith Morgan, the most pink of business partners. Steve and I both remember the day you walked down the hallway of The Acacia as a Money Gym client – and what an effect you have had. Our 'iron fist in a velvet glove' you are always kind & abundant, always loyal & tolerant and always very, very honest. A brain as sharp as a razor and a way with a (large pink) calculator that puts me to shame. Steve and I don't know what we would have done without you.

The Money Gym clients, thousands of you now, and you are all successes in our eyes – as long as you don't give up! Our strategic partners and those who ask me to speak for them, Brett McFall & Tom Hua, the World Internet Summit team, Alan Forrest Smith, Mark Anastasi, Martin Avis, Neil Asher, Daniel Priestley of Triumphant Events, and not to mention the Internet Marketer's Cruise Poker Champion, 'Rebel Aussie Businesswoman' Jennie Armato.

My wonderful children Phoebe & Nelson – what can I say, you are my greatest achievements - just by being you. Love you loads even while you drive me demented.

And last but never least...

Joe Gregory from Bookshaker.com – a great editor who took this book which had been languishing for a year or two, and turned it around so quickly my head spun. It's a dream come true for a girl who had to pay to enter her English 'O level. He's done such a great job. And, too, many thanks to the magical Debbie Jenkins from LeanMarketingPress.com for making it all happen so effortlessly and for putting up with my ADD.

Foreword

As I spend most of my waking life involved with money, finance and wealth creation in some shape and form, it was inevitable really that I would eventually meet Nicola, which I did in around 2001. I am proud to say that we soon became firm friends and colleagues, co-mentors and support coaches for one another.

So when Nicola asked me to write the foreword to this book on the Money Gym I, of course, immediately said yes.

So I sat down to write and unusually for me I got stuck. The responsibility for writing for myself – which I do copiously every single day – is quite different to writing something for somebody else. I struggled with creating a fantastic opener – should I go for a quote from Shakespeare – or perhaps something more contemporary, surely Kiyosaki at the least?

And then it dawned on me – I should just it tell it like it is, so here goes.

This book is partly about Nicola and her journey through wealth creation but more importantly for you as a reader, this book is a template for anybody who wants to create wealth, as it takes you through all the major steps you need to follow.

I have seen many people in my wealth creating career and the vast majority of them are frightened by money and how it impacts their lives – it is the universal excuse for lack of action – what balderdash! What stops people taking action is the fear of moving out of their comfort zones combined with the lack of belief that change will produce results for them.

So to help you address that, this book will tell you the path to take and what to do, hence eliminating many of the fears and challenges you are wrestling with. You don't have to worry about the next step, you just follow the instructions, which are a logical and gradual flow through the financial intelligence arena.

So this book is a guide, and a helper: it is a route map and an action plan; it is a work book and it is an emotional support. It ensures that you set and follow a targeted action plan which is specific and relevant for you.

Nicola is a brave and abundant woman, who has been through her own, sometimes difficult, wealth journey, but having learned the lessons herself she now gives generously of her time, beliefs and energy to me as a friend and colleague and to all who encounter her – including you! There is no better teacher and mentor than Nicola and I am sure that whatever your financial 'challenge' there will be some guidance in this book for you now.

With Nicola's help, this book will help you break through some of the traditional and 'accepted' limitations and boundaries to financial intelligence and take you through many exciting topics such as financial flows, compounding, and investing – I am excited by that even now despite many years of financial awareness and freedom in my own life and I am envious of you if this is new to you – what a fantastic journey you have – and there is no better guide for you than this.

This book not only says you can... it shows you how!

Gill Fielding,
Star of Channel 4's 'Secret Millionaire'

Introduction

Welcome to The Money Gym community. You have made a great decision to buy this book, one that will most probably change the way you think about, and relate to money forever!

This book, based on my Money Gym coaching programmes, workshops and training courses, will show you step by step how to build and develop your own financial intelligence. It's focused on nine core tried and tested Wealth Creation modules:

1. **Discovery** do you know where you are now?

2. **Beliefs, Behaviours & Attitudes** what's holding you back? And where did those beliefs come from?

3. **Cashflow** how it comes in, why and how it goes out

4. **Debt Busting!** stop the rot and sort it forever

5. **Savings –v– Investment & Compounding** why you have to know the difference & the 8th wonder of the world

6. **Equities** a nice little earner on a couple of hours a year

7. **Property Investment** tried and tested throughout the ages

8. **Profit from Your Passion!** harness the power of the internet, make money while you sleep

9. **Mind Your Own Business!** if you want to look in the mirror and see the boss

Why, you may be thinking, do I prefer to say financial intelligence rather than get rich, wealth creation or millionaire thinking? I prefer to use those words rather than anything more flamboyant, because:

1. In the early days, many people don't want to be wealthy or become a millionaire – that's too big and scary!

2. I like to teach people how to fish, slowly and surely, rather than throwing them into a big reservoir full of fish and saying 'there you are – go get it!'

I'm going to help you develop a positive and intelligent way to think about money so that you can go forward with confidence, holding the right tools and possessing the knowledge to improve your life – and those of your family and friends – forever. With your enhanced

'Financial Intelligence' you get to choose what to do with it and why – rather than relying on someone else for answers.

So Who On Earth Is Nicola Cairncross?

I am a very ordinary person – a mother of two who got to the age of 38 completely clueless about money. I went on a quest to find out how money works, and what makes the difference between rich people and poor people and that quest led me to become a Wealth Coach working with bright, successful, professional people who want to:

- Profit from their passion and develop passive income

- Make the leap to self–employed or business owner

- Learn how to become financially free

I usually do that via The Money Gym, my speaking engagements or my Internet Marketing Mentoring programme 'Hidden Star To Superstar'. I have two partners in The Money Gym, Judith Morgan, one of our original ex-clients, and Steve Watson, brilliant chef turned brilliant web designer, and who I met when he used to run my favourite restaurant and then my boutique hotel (you'll hear more about the hotel as we go along).

For many people who have read this book, joined our community, enjoyed coaching with us, or come along to our events, The Money Gym has quite literally changed their lives. It's changed mine, and Judith's and Steve's too.

But why should you listen to me about wealth creation at all? As we go through this book you will find out a bit more about my journey from that 38 year old, unable to pay the rent, with two small children and a husband who had just been made redundant.

Well, I was once one of those serial employees/ entrepreneurs, always madly busy making money for other people but not quite getting there for myself.

Since then I have owned a boutique hotel on the Sussex coast which I bought 'no money down' (and I don't recommend you try that one at home children!), I had a music industry internet company ArtistManager that made me money while I sleep, I'm a property investor (having learned how to buy UK houses for £1) and as I say, I now co-own the Money Gym business and spend most of my days writing, speaking on wealth creation, business success, internet marketing and continually nurturing and adding to the community of wonderful people around us.

But most of all, I can choose my working hours and have time to enjoy my children (usually taking most of the school holidays off!).

I am totally dedicated to enabling other people to undergo the same transformation I went through, by working through this book and getting support from our Money Gym community. I can teach you – in a fun, easy way – the things I have learned, and support you to make the changes that will transform your financial life.

Whatever your financial goals, this book will enable you to learn all the things you were never taught at school and create an effective way for you to become financially free.

This book came about because I wanted to reach more people with the knowledge we share in The Money Gym™. While no book can entirely replace the interactive approach of coaching nor the sense of community of my programmes, it *will* give you a solid grounding in everything you need to know to develop greater financial intelligence. It could even make you rich – if that's what you want. Many people who have read this book have emailed me their stories and I love to hear from readers. You can come along and join us, commenting on any aspect of wealth creation on our blog at *www.TheMoneyGym.com/blog*.

I was originally going to call this book 'Running On Empty'. For a while I thought that would make a great title because I realised a while ago, when people are operating out of a scarcity mentality, as I did for years, they think that by delaying filling up their car with petrol, they will be saving themselves money.

Not true of course, you use as much petrol as you use, and all you are achieving is stress, worrying about whether your car is going to run out of petrol and stop working. All that energy wasted! Try filling up when you are half full, (not half empty – note!) rather than when you are on the red line. It will make a difference in your life and the way you think, I guarantee it!

Then I realised that it was just too negative. And while I'm a realist, I do believe amazing things can happen when you change your mind set from 'glass half empty' to 'glass half full'. So my great title had to go, and I chose something that said what it does on the tin. I'm a great believer in calling your business something that says what it does on the tin as you will find out in the internet marketing chapter 'Profit From Your Passion'.

This is a personal workout programme that will build your financial fitness by encouraging you to take action, make things happen and test what I'm sharing first hand. I like to keep things down to earth and practical. That way you'll be able to sort your finances out, once and for all.

I have read all the business and wealth creation books out there, and I still do, and I've pulled out all the good stuff, put it to the test and I only share the 'wisdom that works' in this book. I've read all this stuff so you don't have to – but I would still recommend you do, however! You will find my recommended reading list at the end of this book.

I really hope you enjoy it and that things get as good as they can be for you as a result! I would love to know how you get on so feel free to email me at *nicola@themoneygym.com.*

But before we go any further, here is a blank 'Workout Plan' for you to use. You'll find one of these at the end of each chapter in this book. I always found that I loved to read 'self–help' books but the minute I started to do the exercises, make notes in the margins, and underline things, my life started to change. It's totally unrecognisable now.

So to make the most of this book, as you read each chapter, make notes of your desired personal action steps in the spaces provided.

I have also included a 'Desired Outcome' sheet for you to fill in before you go any further. Make a copy and take two minutes to fill it in. It should evolve as you work through the book so remember to keep it updated!

Do all this, work through the next nine modules, take some action and your financial life *will* begin to change for the better.

Nicola Cairncross
www.TheMoneyGym.com/blog
www.NicolaCairncross.com/blog

THE MONEY GYM WORKOUT PLAN

These are the actions I will take in the next month, arising from
Module #

1. _____

2. _____

3. _____

4. _____

5. _____

6. _____

7. _____

8. _____

9. _____

10. _____

11. _____

12. _____

13. _____

14. _____

15. _____

16. _____

17. _____

18. _____

19. _____

20. _____

Signed: _____ Date: _____

THE MONEY GYM
DESIRED OUTCOME WORKSHEET

Name: _____

My objective for reading this book is to:

_____

_____

_____

_____

_____

_____

_____

_____

My definition of wealth is:

_____

_____

_____

_____

_____

_____

_____

_____

_____

_____

Signed: _____ Date: _____

The Things You Need To Know...

If you take each section of this book, within each chapter, you could use it as a day by day plan and aim to just read a section a day, let it sink in, then read the next section. If you DO work through this book using the day to day system, then you will increase your Financial Intelligence dramatically within just 90 days, especially if you take action.

But there's nothing stopping you reading from start to finish now, to fill in all the knowledge, and then take things at your own pace afterwards. It's your book so do what feels right.

On another point, many of the sections contain a key lesson drawn directly from the wealth of material included in The Money Gym Coaching Programmes™. This is the first time such exclusive material has been made available in such an accessible format *and* at such an affordable price. So don't let your small investment fool you into not taking action – this stuff works.

Exercises

Occasionally an exercise will be suggested; I would recommend that you do the exercises as they come up, but you can also wait until the end of the module and do them all together.

Book Recommendations

As we go along, I will also include book recommendations and the most important resources available on the web today, to help you move forward in your quest for Financial Freedom.

** BONUS FREE REPORTS **

I have created some very special bonus free reports for you including 'How To Become A Millionaire Within Five Years', 'Natural Marketing For Lone Rangers' and 'Business Success 21st Century Style'. All you have to do to enjoy those reports is to join my mailing list by following the instructions here: *www.TheMoneyGym.com/freereports*

Action Steps

I will be suggesting actions to take, which will move you forward. This book will have an effect on your thinking even if you ignore the action steps. But boy, will it have an even greater effect if you actually take them! This is what they look like and here's your first one...

ACTION STEP

What can you do to get ready for the rest of the life-changing information in this book?

Complete this statement, 'I will feel wealthy when...' with as many items as you can.

Then take another piece of paper and complete this statement, 'I ALREADY feel wealthy when...' Again, push yourself to fill it in as many times as you can.

When you have completed this exercise congratulate yourself. You have already shown yourself to be very different from the 95% of people who read books, attend seminars and... ...do nothing.

Read them again. Interesting, aren't they? We'll come back to those later in the book. Keep them safe.

My Bold Promise!

If you follow the Money Gym book step by step, if you do the exercises included, if you read the books recommended and then TAKE ACTION, within 90 days you will have dramatically improved the way you think about money, interact with money, and feel about money forever.

I will go even further: If you do all this, you will also find that you will start to make more money, keep more money, make money while you sleep and make your existing money work for you. You will feel more confident about the decisions you make and feel so much happier about your financial future than you ever have before.

How can I possibly make this promise? Because it happened to me. It's happened to many, many Money Gym clients. And now, it could happen for you. So let's get started on the first chapter!

CHAPTER 1
Discovery

Why Do We Bother?

Are you one of those people who earn well but don't know where your money goes every month? Perhaps you make money for your company or boss but yearn to be self–employed. Do you ever get the nagging feeling that your money should be working for you rather than you always having to work for your money?

You're not alone!

That was me in 1998, just a few years ago. I used to gaze at my wage slip willing it to change, willing the net sum earned to get bigger, as if by magic and willpower and wishing I could MAKE it grow. I sensed that there was more to this 'money business' than met the eye. It was almost as if there was a secret key, that I didn't have, to unlock the answers to money management and wealth creation.

So... would you like the good news or the bad news first?

The good news is that people who can 'handle money' have access to a few key pieces of knowledge that many people will never know. Perhaps they learned these tricks from a family member, taught themselves, or just 'knew it in their bones'. However they came by it doesn't matter; you're going to learn their tricks too.

The bad news? There's no secret key or magic wand. Sorry. You will have to stop waiting for that knight in shining armour, windfall or lottery win. If you really want things to change for the better, *you* will have to take some action and, little by little, start to change your beliefs, behaviours and attitudes around money.

SO WHY DO IT AT ALL?

The first important thing is to find your motivation. You can pay any number of experts to help you out, but at the end of the day it's down to you. **No–one will EVER care as much about your financial well–being as you do.**

Just think about how it would feel to:

- Work just because you want to
- Make confident financial decisions
- Never have to answer to anyone again

How great would it be to:

- Listen to the news knowing that you are unlikely to be affected by redundancy
- Make life choices based on other criteria than whether you can 'afford' it
- Feel strong and supported with a financial cushion behind you
- Give back to your community in some way and make a difference

---

ACTION STEP

The 'Tuesday' Exercise

Write down how you would like to be living your life, on a Tuesday in two, five and ten year's time. Write down where you are, who you are with and what you are doing from the moment you get up to the moment you go to bed. Is it compelling enough yet?

If not, go back to it again and again and build a vivid and specific scene. See your life when you are a success, feel how you feel, smell the smells and specifically, feel the emotions, the joy, the happiness and above all, the gratitude.

Here are some questions to get you started:

- Where do you live?
- What do you live in?
- Who are your friends?
- What hobbies do you have and how often do you do them?
- What do you do for personal fulfilment?
- Describe your relationship with your significant other / children. How much time you spend together and what do you do together?
- How many hours a day do you work?
- When do you work?
- What do you do when you are working?
- What are you responsible for?
- What are your clients / customers like?

- Describe your work environment
- Talk about your team (nobody makes it alone by the way)
- What about what you do makes you proud?
- What time you wake up?
- How, where, what and with who do you spend the morning?
- How, where, what and with who do you spend the afternoon?
- How, where, what and with who do you spend the evening?

TIP: If you struggle with this exercise, one of the most important in the book, it sometimes helps to reverse the questions and start with what you don't want!

WEALTH WARNING!

Thinking of skipping this exercise? That's the first hurdle most people fall at. Many people read all the books and attend all the courses yet they never take action and wonder why things are just the same. The first step to taking action in the big wide world is to do the exercises in this book.

So, if you think that this step is pie in the sky and can be bypassed, be warned; if you can't be bothered to do *this* properly, you will probably never be able to create financial abundance for yourself.

Successful people take the time to create powerful visions for themselves. It makes the goal setting so much more fun and takes away the need for 'self–discipline'.

'Once you define your ideal day, you'll immediately find being more aware of your priorities puts things in perspective. Focusing on a brighter future, like your ideal life, pulls you towards it. Focusing on an ideal future relaxes the mind and helps you to respond correctly (not react) to whatever situations come your way'

Rich Schefren 'Your Business Blueprint'
www.StrategicProfits.com

What Are The Four Lanes of the Wealth Superhighway

This huge feeling of relief washed over me when I realised that there are just four ways to create real, lasting, sustainable wealth – a bit like the four lanes on a motorway. I'll be going into each of the four lanes of the wealth highway in more detail later on but, for the moment, think to yourself, 'Phew!' that's not too overwhelming – anyone can learn about just four things!

Those four lanes are:

1. Property Investment (at least 10 ways to invest in property)

2. The Stockmarket (exposure to equities in some form or other)

3. Minding Your Own Business (even if you have a job)

4. Profiting From Your Passion (creating passive revenue streams while you sleep)

Each lane has a myriad of vehicles to ride in – perhaps a pushbike will suit you better than a juggernaut initially and maybe you will want more than one vehicle in each lane!

Each vehicle will produce different results in terms of outcomes – are you looking for results while you travel (income) or slow steady travel (growth) that gets you there in the end?

We all have our preferred driving styles. Which is yours? Decide if you are a pushbike person or a Ferrari person. Both will get you there but one will be faster. Think about which lane of the motorway you are going to drive down first – and no, you don't have to get a vehicle on all of them to start with, but you can be aware that the more vehicles you have on each lane, the faster you will get to your destination.

So what is your destination? Where are you now? Because one thing is for sure, if you don't know where you are now financially, you are less likely to be able to get to your destination successfully.

Because... well, think about it for a moment. If you don't know where you are now, you are LOST, are you not?

If you are trying to get to Manchester, but you don't know where you are starting out from, you are much less likely to get decent directions!

Now, think about how big and powerful a vehicle you would like on each lane, or whether you would feel more comfortable with a myriad of little vehicles on each lane.

What kind of a driver are you?

Self Discipline -v- Simplicity

I don't actually believe in self–discipline. I believe in creating a compelling vision, setting chunked–down goals with timelines, setting things up so that they are as easy to achieve as possible and then designing environments and support systems to ensure your success.

We have talked a bit about the compelling vision and the next thing to consider is simplicity.

The secret to financial success is to KISS (keep it simple, smarty!).

I have tried every accounting package under the sun (Microsoft Money worked for a while) but they are all just too complicated. You don't need all that stuff! A simple Excel spreadsheet that tracks your bank account and feeds into an 18 month cashflow forecast will do the job nicely.

I have an Excel spreadsheet already set up for this purpose. If you'd like a copy then come along to The Money Gym Blog and join Money Gym Silver for the 30-day free trial, then you can download it from the Cashflow section (Module 3).

Learn how to use Excel fast. Nothing fancy, just a few simple basics. Try the tutorial, buy a book – there must be an 'Excel for Dummies' book - or get a local computer–savvy teenager in for a few hours to show you how to set up a simple formula to add rows of figures up, so that if you change one of the figures, the total changes.

Every week, I take my cashflow forecast, which is set up to predict my income and outgoings weekly, not monthly and I compare it to what has happened in my bank account, from a printout from my internet banking.

I bold the items that actually happened, until the carried forward total matches the amount in my bank account up to that point, then I carry forward any items that I predicted but that haven't happened.

This feeds through into a simple set of management accounts which also tell me what my income tax provision and VAT payable should be. I move those sums into my business deposit account.

Then the next week I do the same. Don't overcomplicate things.

This technique enables me to know the impact that every bill, every cash-point withdrawal, every amount earned, will have on my finances up to 18 months time. I can see any potential problems in plenty of time to do something about them.

And that brings financial peace of mind which is a pearl without price.

13

My first wealth mentor, property investor and C4 Secret Millionaire Gill Fielding, always used to say that if your finances can't be fitted onto a simple spreadsheet, it ain't working. I also once worked for an entrepreneur who said that if a deal couldn't be demonstrated on the back of a fag packet it was no good. Gill's finances are very sophisticated in terms of ease of use and earning power but very simply laid out. Just a simple spreadsheet. Don't make it harder for yourself – force yourself to keep it almost baby–like.

Pull It All Together

The oil that lubricates your money–making vehicles is information. How can you make good decisions if you don't have all the information you need at your fingertips? Here is where we gather everything you will need into one place. Don't worry! You don't have to do anything with it just yet.

ACTION STEP

First of all, gather **The Equipment**. You will need a ring binder or two, some coloured file dividers (minimum of 5), plastic wallets to keep small items and loose sheets in, a hole punch and a stapler. You also need three pens; black, red and blue or green. Gather everything together first, because if you need to get up from your seat for anything, you will get distracted by the kettle, the washing or the cat etc, and will lose the momentum.

Next, gather **The Information**. Recent bank statements, credit card statements, wage slips or sales invoices (if you are self employed). Put Tax Stuff in a separate pile.

File the bank statements at the front section, in date order, with oldest items at the back. Credit card statements similarly.

Next the 'money in' section, wage slips or invoices. Then the 'money out' section. Receipts or invoices for things you buy. How much you divide each section up is entirely up to you – again, keep it simple to start with.

Get a printout from the bank of all current direct debits or standing orders.

Wealth Building Exercise: Your Financial Table

You now have all the information to be ready to complete the Financial Table. You may not be able to complete this yet but don't panic! Hold onto it until you feel ready.

It *is* important as it will create a financial snapshot of where you are now. And if you don't know where you are now, how will you know if you're making any progress in the future?

If the worst comes to the worst, just put in an estimation of your current net worth, and then fill in a figure for your ideal future net worth.

If you do feel able to tackle it, this is how you go about it.

THE '£ NOW' COLUMN: Go down the list of headings and fill in the current value of your assets (the hoorays) and liabilities (the boos).

You can find values on the annual statements you receive and if you don't have these phone the customer help desk of your provider and ask for a statement to be sent. All financial service providers will be very happy to do this and it is a very common request. If I haven't included your specific category then there is room at the bottom to add your own categories.

Add up all your assets and total all your debts or liabilities. Then deduct the debts from the assets to get your total net worth.

When I did this for the first time I amazed myself. I thought I would be in negative net worth and I found out that I was actually worth £16k more than I thought I was. I had forgotten two endowment policies that I had taken out years before. This wealth coaching stuff works, I thought! I felt wealthier already!

THE '£ FUTURE' COLUMN: It was a big surprise to me that you *can* estimate what you will be worth at some point in the future (you choose, it can be one year, three years, five years or even ten years away).

If you assume that different types of investment appreciate on average at a certain percentage, year on year, you can work it out. If you have an asset worth, say, £10,000, and you know that this kind of asset appreciates at about 10% per year, then by the end of year one it will be worth £11,000. By the end of year three it will be worth £13,310, year five £16,105 and year ten £25,937.

	£ NOW	£ FUTURE
ASSETS		
House		
Car		
PEP / TESSA / ISA		
Building Society Account		
Investment properties		
Investment Club		
Unit Trust or Investment Trust holdings		
Equities or shares		
Endowments and insurance policies		
Pensions		
Valuables		
Cash at the bank		
Cash under the bed		
Antiques		
Jewellery		
Other valuables and assets		
SUB TOTAL (ASSETS)		
LIABILITIES		
House mortgage(s)		
Business loans		
Private loans		
Credit Card Debt		
Hire Purchase		
Account card debt (e.g. shop cards)		
Loans from friends and family		
Overdue bills		
Other loans and debts		
Sub Total (Liabilities)		
GRAND TOTAL – NET WORTH	£	£

Can I Have A Receipt, Please?

Receipts fill in the knowledge gaps between your bank and credit card statements – especially if you make a lot of cash withdrawals.

Think about it, if you sat down for one morning at the end of each month, you would be able to tell what you had spent by direct debit or standing order, cheque or cash (but only if you had the cash receipts).

Try to get into the habit of paying by debit card (unless you are trying to stick to a budget by taking out a fixed amount of cash per week and living on that) as it lists the shop name on your bank statement and helps you figure out what you spent where.

But if you can't use a debit card and like to use 'real' money, then just ask for a receipt for absolutely everything you buy, no matter how little.

Self–employed people are usually pretty good at doing this for their business, but it often never occurs to them to run their personal finances like a business too.

Don't worry for the time being about what to do with all of these pieces of paper, just collect them.

Get into the habit of asking for a receipt for every purchase you make. It's easier to ask for a receipt every time, than trying to remember what you need receipts for (or not). Tuck them immediately inside your purse, an envelope in your bag, or a plastic wallet in your filofax. Just have one place in your bag, purse or coat where you put every receipt you get.

Then, at the end of the day, empty it out into just one place in your home or office. Once a week, move them into one of the plastic wallets in your lever arch file. Label the wallet 'Receipts – w/e' and put the date.

And then forget about them (for the time being).

I'll Just Get The File Out

Mark Forster, bestselling author on time management, says that when you tend to procrastinate about doing essential tasks, the best thing to say to yourself is 'I'll just get the file out'.

I will go one further here, and ask you to think to yourself, 'when, each week, is the best time for me to just get the file out?' Unless you schedule some regular time to look at your finances, you will never get round to it, the receipts will pile up and it will swiftly become a psychologically insurmountable task.

But schedule some time you must and find a way to make it enjoyable. Make yourself a nice cappuccino to sip while you work. Put on some classical music (Bach is supposed to be the best music for aiding concentration). Ask a buddy round to help you.

Make it nice, make it fun, but find a way to make sure you do it. Your future financial success depends on getting into good habits now.

Start slowly. Don't expect to be able to change the habits of a lifetime overnight. If you can just get into the habit of collecting the information you need and keeping it tidy, you have all the tools at your fingertips for when you are ready to move to the next stage.

Make Time. If you schedule some time each week, you should be able to do everything required to become a financial whiz kid in about 2 hours maximum. Sunday or Monday mornings are good, so are Monday evenings. Perhaps you want to take a day off to get started? Or use that dead week between Christmas and New Year. So when *are* YOU going to 'just get the file out'?

Get support. You could talk to your partner, spouse, etc. and tell them how you want to get a handle on your money, and tell them the time you have set aside to do it. Ask for their support, by not distracting you or tempting you with offers of 'more exciting' things to do. I promise, as your financial intelligence increases, as you take more action, as your wealth creation gathers pace, this will swiftly become one of those 'more exciting' things – that allows you to do even more 'more exciting' things.

Saving -v- Investing

I never understood the point of saving. What did you save for? Things you were going to buy later? Why not have them now? I didn't understand the difference between saving and investing. And with the low interest rates for savings I couldn't see the point. I totally didn't get the power of compounding.

Nobody told me that it isn't what you earn that counts, it isn't what you spend even, that counts. What really counts is what you keep.

Nobody said that the reason wealthy people are wealthy is because they are taught to put an extra step (like a fuel filter if you like) in between the action of 'earning' and the action of 'spending'. That extra step is investing. Investing in assets that produce income all by themselves.

Then in 1998 I saw a drawing that changed my life. It explained the point of saving to invest. I saw the power of compounding in one little drawing.

It was in a book called 'Swimming With Piranha Makes You Hungry' by Colin Turner. Right near the end of the book.   I had to read that book five times to actually SEE that drawing but I finally did.

It blew my mind. And here it is:

Financial Freedom: A Picture

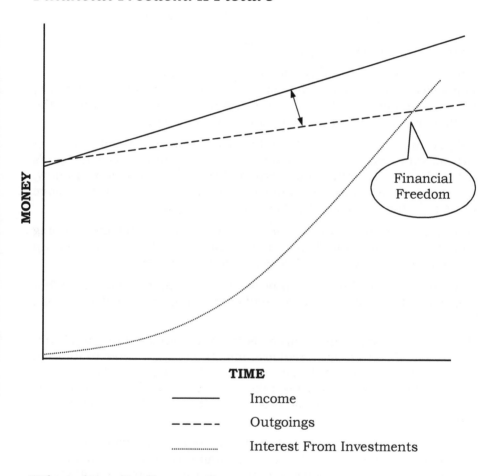

What does it all mean?

The solid line is your income, the dashed line your outgoings, the black arrow being the difference between the two (what you keep) and the dotted line the interest your savings (or other investments) can earn you taking into account the power of compounding.

When the dotted line crosses the dashed line – you are financially free. Forget the million, it can be as soon as you like. The bigger the gap between your income and outgoings, the faster the dotted line will climb to cross your dashed line.

Why does it climb so steeply? You are watching the beauty of appreciation (or interest) building on appreciation (or interest).

It's compounding (more on that subject later) at work.

Take Your Financial Driving Test

You wouldn't expect to get in a car, never having driven before, blindfolded, no seatbelt, hanging your legs out of the window, drinking champagne, driving the wrong way up the motorway in the wrong lane and not end up in a car crash, would you?

Well, so many people take their first excursion into wealth creation with no skills, no training, no advice and no mentor or coach. So it's no wonder they usually come a cropper! How many folk do you know, who buy a share on the stock market based on a hot tip from a bloke in the pub, then wonder why they end up losing money?

How many people leave their job and start a business doing something they loved to do as a hobby, then wonder why they end up as one of the 85% whose business fails in the first year?

How many people invest in 'buy to let' then wonder why their 'hot property' sits empty or worse, ends up being 'squatted' by a bad tenant?

The key to this financial malarkey is to know yourself. First of all, you must know if you are an impulsive, impetuous type, liable to jump in feet first and give up if it doesn't work first time. Or perhaps you are a more cautious soul who never takes action unless you know all the facts and figures and have the proof in front of you? So you never take action at all.

The other reason that you must know yourself, is that you can choose your road to wealth to suit your personality type. I have mentioned that I never saved because the interest rates were so pathetic, I figured that on the amount I could afford to save, I'd be dead before I had accumulated enough money to be comfortable, let alone wealthy. Typical savings rates are between 4–6% nowadays if you put it in a building society.

Would you be amazed if I told you that Business Angels, investing in fledgling startup companies, expect around a 30–35% return on their money *year on year*? And their money back!

Would you be amazed if I told you that I met a property investor who won't invest in a property unless he gets a 100% return on his money year on year? And that is based on just rental income, not capital appreciation.

Decide which lane of the wealth highway you are going to tackle first. Get a book, take some training, find a mentor – get started – by all means as quickly and inexpensively as possible, but get help!

I recently went on a property investment course that cost £1880. Expensive? I learnt two things that made me a minimum of £40,000. Starting to look cheap now! You *can* learn this stuff and you should be ready to invest in training in the same way you paid for your driving lessons. And if you are finding yourself resisting that idea, think about the hot tips from the bloke in the pub. How good is 'free advice' really if it ends up costing you money with an expensive mistake?

Usually the reason it's free is because it's absolutely worthless!

ACTION STEP

Pull out all the loose change in your pocket, and work out how much you would have in 10 years, if you achieved a 100% return on your small change, year on year, for 10 years. Doubling your money, every year, in effect.

Perhaps you are more interested in saving to invest now? Starting to find some motivation to find a way to 'liberate' some cash, to put it to work for you?

Would you be interested in finding out how to achieve a 35%–100% return on your money? Well, you are in the right place. We are going to cover that later in this book.

Your Wealth Team

Though the bloke in the pub may be full of useless advice (which is why it's free!), there are people worth listening to.

Find a great bank manager – usually a business bank manager rather than a personal manager. Imagine how many businesses they see per week – they see the good and the bad, the ones who are successful despite themselves and the ones that fail even though the idea is good.

My bank manager, who was Mike Murray, from NatWest Bank in Worthing, was a brilliant bloke. He was generous with his time in spite of the pressures on him and I knew I was onto a winner when he told me he had a drawer full of business ideas himself. He's now a seasoned property investor, owns a successful coffee shop in Worthing and is looking forward to a very comfortable retirement indeed.

A good accountant can help you set things up well for you before you even start. Mark Nicholson, from Spofforths in Worthing, set up my companies in such a way (legally!) that I will save a great deal of tax. I would never in a million years have known what he knows. I can't recommend Mark highly enough – 10 years on!

A great solicitor will help you avoid legal problems you may not even know about.

I now have many wealth creation 'buddies' and mentors – people who are more financially successful than I am and who love to talk about what they are up to. Inspirational, knowledgeable, supportive, aspirational, and they love to share what they know. One of my old friends, who was very wealthy indeed and inspired me tremendously, told me once that she used to write shopping lists that include 'pick the dry cleaning up', 'see Mum' and 'have Mercedes Soft Top by 30 yrs'.

And when I think I might never have met Gill Fielding – well, I just shudder at the thought.

In the same way, avoid people who are negative about everything or who are 'energy vampires'. They will come out of the woodwork as you become more interested in wealth creation and finance and it always amazes me how much energy they will put into trying to discredit what you are learning about or trying to do, rather than improving their own lives!

There is even one chap in the USA who has a website devoted to investigating Russ Whitney and Robert Allen (two famous wealth creation gurus) – I have to wonder why doesn't he get on with his own wealth creation instead of trying to debunk others?

ACTION STEP

Make a list of all of the people you spend significant amounts of time with.

Work colleagues, friends, family and anyone else you may network with. Put a tick next to their name if they are positive, supportive and successful in their own right. Use your own definition of success here. Start to identify who could be in your Wealth Team and begin to ask some searching questions.

If you want to get involved in Property Investment for example, then ask everyone you meet (and particularly everyone you are thinking of including in your Wealth Team) these kind of questions. Are you a Property Investor? How many properties do you have? What is your investment strategy (just means plan)?

If you are interested in starting your own business, ask them if they have any other businesses on the side, what are they, what the plan is for that business? If they answer in the negative, go and find people who are involved and already active in what you want to do. Surround yourself with action orientated people.

Why would they talk to you and tell you their business? Because successful people have an abundance mentality, that's why. They love to share what they know, and learn from other people. For all they know, you may be able to teach them something new! And you will, one day.

The Magic Wand

So you are still with us then! I bet you couldn't wait for this part of the book! The Magic Wand.

So the magic wand! What is that all about? Oh, if only there was one.

When I was a little girl I really, really believed that I was a princess in disguise and that, soon, my real parents (a king and queen obviously!) would come and reclaim me. Then, as I got older, I was convinced that a prince would recognise my innate royalty and elevate me to the financial life I aspired to.

Well, eventually the truth dawned on me. Sorry, there *are* no magic wands, no knights in shining armour. And then I realised that if I was going to achieve my financial potential, it was down to me. And how much time had I wasted already? Babe, I said to myself, you will just have to take some action.

But I consoled myself with the thought that doing something 30 times makes it a habit. If you just ask for a receipt 30 times it will become second nature. If you 'just get the file out' 30 times, you will be in the habit of sitting down to spend some time on your money. If you ask 29 people if they are property investors and they all say no, chances are the 30th will say yes.

Above all, I reminded myself not to give up if it seems overwhelming. Just get help. Take a class, attend a weekend seminar or get a coach <grin>.

So I did, and the happy ending is coming faster than I dreamed possible. Since I started this process, I have accelerated my financial growth dramatically over the last three years – catching up for 20 years of waiting for the prince, the king and queen, the knight in shining armour.

I'm busy polishing my own armour and all of my crowns now! And you can too.

Play games with wealth creation. We are going to go into all of this in a lot more detail, but get creative. Draw a grid for each debt with a square for every repayment you will make on each debt and colour each square in every time a standing order goes off.

Buy the brilliant board game, invented by Robert Kiyosaki, Cashflow 101 and practice wealth creation with pretend money first! Or come along to one of The Money Gym's Cashflow days – you can find out more about our events at www.TheMoneyGym.com/blog

Join an investment club (more about that in the Equities module) and make money while making new friends.

The more fun this is, the more likely you are to take action.

Find a buddy who is into this wealth creation malarkey as much as you are, and get your partner/spouse on your side and excited about the possibilities of financial freedom for them too.

Find a mentor or get a coach, one who is actually doing the things you aspire to do now.

But whatever you do, do something!

THE MONEY GYM WORKOUT PLAN

These are the actions I will take in the next month, arising from Module 1: Discovery

1. _____

2. _____

3. _____

4. _____

5. _____

6. _____

7. _____

8. _____

9. _____

10. _____

11. _____

12. _____

13. _____

14. _____

15. _____

16. _____

17. _____

18. _____

19. _____

20. _____

Signed: _____ Date: _____

CHAPTER 2
Beliefs, Behaviours & Attitudes

Don't Keep It In The Family

For the last 40 years or so I've had a deep conviction that I was going to be a successful business person one day. I didn't even know what a successful business person actually did but I knew I wanted to be one. I also knew that I was really a princess in disguise but you already know that story!

But over the last five or ten years a nagging feeling grew that perhaps I had been made with a fatal flaw inside me that would stop the success from ever happening.

What I didn't realise was that success doesn't just happen. You have to make it happen.

How do you do that?

By deciding what you want to do and finding out what you need to know, in order to do it. Seems obvious doesn't it?

But what if what you want to do is to make money? For whatever reason, you just don't seem to be able to do that. Well, the first place to look is your family. We have talked about expectations, and the next thing to examine is how your family related to money. Where did you inherit your beliefs about money? We tend to follow the beliefs, behaviours and attitudes of the folks around us. Consider your parents and relatives attitudes to money.

What kind of people were your parents? Did your family pass on the assumption that you worked hard, earned and saved for retirement? How did they both relate to money? Was your mum different to your dad on this? Did they fight about money or just not talk about it in front of you? Was one entrepreneurial while the other was cautious? Which one do you take after? What about uncles, aunts, grandparents. Who had the biggest influence on you, where money is concerned?

When I thought about this, the one key phrase I remember being bandied about in my house was, 'we can't afford it'. As soon as I changed that into, 'how could I afford it?' things started to change for me, dramatically. The other was, 'you can have anything you want in life as long as you want it badly enough and work hard enough' – guess what effect that had on me!

Write down the one main statement that was true about how your parents related to the subject of money, around you. Now write down how that has translated into how you feel about, and deal with money, yourself.

Abundance -v- Scarcity

A turning point for me came when I realised that there was enough money sloshing around the world for every single person to have in excess of £1 million. It's out there, somewhere, and who is to say that I am not as equally deserving of some of it, as the next person?

Do you ever complain that you don't earn enough? Why is that? Is it that your company pays everyone the same as you?

No? So why is it that your company pays someone else more than you? 'But they won't pay *me* any more!' you may say. What is the difference between you and the higher paid person? Is there so much difference between you and that other person?

Hmm, that's an interesting thought isn't it?

And it leads onto the thought, 'well, what would it take for me to become the kind of person who is paid more for what I do?'

What made me leave school and apply for low to medium paid jobs? Why were my expectations so much lower than those of a similar child, same height, same hair colour, same IQ? What made them certain that they deserved to be a lawyer, a singer or a doctor while I was thinking about working in an office or becoming a hairdresser?

I can tell you one thing; if, at the age of 16, I'd known what dentists can earn, especially nowadays, and be self–employed (one of my dreams) then I would have seriously considered dentistry! Why was I still, at 38 years old, as my husband was made redundant, applying for secretarial jobs for £12k– 14k per annum?

Bill Gates is so rich that, if he was a country, he would be the 7th richest country in the world (that may even have changed recently to the 4th richest!). Did he gain his wealth by taking it away from someone else? No, in fact, he made other people richer as well. There is not a finite supply of money – you can create wealth out of nothing. In 2001 I created a company and sold my half of it for over £12,000. £12,000 created out of an idea.

Up until the recent financial crisis, the fact was that banks actually wanted to lend. They actually have lending targets.

When the market recovers, all we will have to do is present our case, our idea, our business, in such a way as to make it easy for them to lend to us. But remember, we only want to borrow to buy assets that will pay for themselves and increase in value, without us having to dig into our pockets.

Gill Fielding says that wealth creation needs the Scales Of Abundance to be in balance. Do you think those Scales are out of whack for most people?

Consider the example of the little old lady who lived so frugally she had lunch in the pub on OAP days to save electricity, but then left millions to the cats' home. Consider the example of the loud flash bloke in the restaurant who dresses well, earns a fortune, drinks Krug and waves a gold or platinum AMEX card about, but who hasn't got an asset to his name.

What is the difference between them? Which is the wealthier? Who has the best beliefs, behaviours and attitudes?

What sets people's expectations at certain levels? Think about where you have set yours and why?

There are some great books on this subject. Try reading 'Think & Grow Rich' by Napoleon Hill or 'Rich Dad's Cashflow Quadrant' by Robert Kiyosaki.

I recommend a great website by Maggy Whitehouse. Maggy works quite deeply on Prosperity Thinking and I am really impressed with her approach to her subject. She has some great tools and games on her site that will take you further with this module.

You can find her at www.pureprosperity.com. Her passion revolves around increasing our abundance by releasing our blockages around money and encouraging us to set our intent. Her site offers loads of great free information including a cheque for One Million Pounds... how handy is that... which you can print off.

Needless to say, this is what I have done, and it now resides above my desk along with my Client List, targets for next year, Treasure Map and Enlightened Millionaire certificate (from the 'One Minute Millionaire' book).

Wealth Building Exercise: Your Beliefs

Examples of Negative Beliefs

- ❑ If only I could get a full time job I would be wealthy
- ❑ If only I could get a pay rise I could sort out my money
- ❑ You have to be born with money to be truly wealthy
- ❑ I'm not smart enough to be wealthy
- ❑ The only way to make money these days is to take risks
- ❑ The only way to make money now is on the Internet
- ❑ All the good ideas for money making are gone
- ❑ I'm too old/too young to be wealthy
- ❑ Money isn't discussed at polite dinner tables
- ❑ The love of money is the root of all evil
- ❑ You have to be nasty to make money
- ❑ People won't like me if I'm wealthy
- ❑ If I'm rich then somebody else will have to be poor, and I don't want that
- ❑ I'm too nice to be wealthy
- ❑ I'd lose all my friends if I had money
- ❑ One day I'll win the lottery or inherit money, or marry money
- ❑ If I were rich I wouldn't be able to go to the same pub/club/gym/school as I do now
- ❑ Neither a borrower nor a lender be
- ❑ I'm not worthy of wealth
- ❑ I'm not good enough to have money
- ❑ If I upset the apple cart of what I have now I might lose it all – i.e. it's too risky
- ❑ Making money isn't nice!
- ❑ Decent, good people don't care about money
- ❑ I'm too scared to take the risk
- ❑ Money won't make me happy
- ❑ You can't be rich in our society because the banks, government, the Inland Revenue, and other people are all out to take it from you
- ❑ Being wealthy means you have to work too hard
- ❑ I'm not disciplined enough to be wealthy
- ❑ You need money to make money

☐ Money just brings problems

Examples of Positive Beliefs

☐ I am worthy

☐ The sea of financial abundance will come to me

☐ Whatever I want/need will come to me

☐ My income will constantly increase

☐ Wealth is a matter of choice

☐ The world and nature are full of abundance

☐ Everything I want is there for when I am ready to collect it

☐ Money is fun

☐ I deserve to live in luxury

☐ I have enough, I am enough

☐ I am wealthy

☐ I will always find a way to finance what I want to do or have

☐ The Inland Revenue is my friend

☐ Wealthy people are fun, happy, generous and kind

☐ Making money is easy

☐ I am in control of my financial flows

☐ Money is positive energy

☐ I am attractive to money, and money is attractive to me

☐ I LOVE money

☐ I embrace wealth

☐ I welcome money with open arms

☐ I am my greatest asset.

☐ I am worthy of any financial investment I can make for myself and the development of ME

☐ I manage my money with pleasure

☐ Money is my friend

☐ Every penny I spend returns to me multiplied

☐ Clients are always happy to pay me

☐ It is easy for me to save and make money

☐ Other people will help me to become wealthy

☐ I receive money easily and effortlessly, achieving great results with the assistance of others

If you cannot tick any of the above positive beliefs, then what's stopping you? If a positive belief is not true for you YET, there is a negative belief hiding behind it. Identify this negative or limiting belief and then work through the following in the same way you would for a negative belief.

Wealth Building Exercise: Your Beliefs

Other examples of my own beliefs are:

```
```

Particularly strong beliefs for me are:

```
```

Beliefs I would like to hold are:

```
```

Collapse each limiting or negative belief:

1. Remind yourself why you want to get rid of the belief i.e. find your <u>motivation</u>!

2. <u>Question</u> that belief. So let's say that your belief is that money isn't fun. Ask yourself:
   a. How does this belief serve me in life?
   b. What does this belief do for me?
   c. What behaviours or actions does this belief create for me that I need to lose?
   d. Is the belief true?
   e. Do I want to get rid of this belief?
   f. When do I want to lose it?
   g. When do I want to start to eradicate it?

3. Have I any <u>evidence</u> from my past where this belief was not true for me? Do I have any experience that contradicts the belief? When was it? What is the evidence?

4. Do I know of <u>anybody</u> for whom this belief is definitely not true? What can I learn from that? What can I copy from that person that will serve me better?

Establish a positive belief:

1. Identify why you want this belief, and what it will give you. Or how it will change your actions or behaviours towards money.

2. Clearly identify the belief as a goal and draw yourself a treasure map for the goal. Put your goal clearly on the paper in the centre and then add around it all your treasures. A treasure map can take many forms but one simple format is to cut out pictures from magazines of things you would buy with your newfound wealth and stick it on a sheet of paper. Or you can stick pictures, or draw pictures, in a book of houses, holidays, cars, share portfolios and so on.

3. Work hard at this treasure map and keep adding to it. As your belief takes hold and you experience behaviour changes add pictures or descriptions of the things you have now been able to afford. Add your own descriptions of how good it feels to be more positive, describe how well you are doing, and give examples of new things you have achieved.

4. You can constantly update or add to these maps and they provide amazing evidence for you in the future as you can see your own progress. They also act as a 'well done' or congratulatory piece of evidence which can be useful if you have a temporary lapse.

5. Write your belief as an affirmation and read through your affirmations last thing at night and first thing in the morning.

6. Practice the belief in the comfort of your own home, and then further–a–field. The idea here is to fake I till you make it! Just pretend that you have the belief already. Get used to how it feels and get comfortable with it.

7. Celebrate your every success on the road to achieving the belief. Reward yourself with treats and acknowledgment, and make this part of your treasure map.

In short, create your own prophesy about your wealth which you then bring into reality.

It's Not What You Earn That Counts!

In fact, I'll go further. It's not what you earn, it's not what you spend, it's what you keep, then what you do with what you keep that counts!

When you play Robert Kiyosaki's brilliant board game, Cashflow 101, you swiftly find out that it's easier to win if you start out as the Janitor than if you draw the Airline Pilot or Doctor card. This is because the Pilot and the Doctor have a lifestyle to support and every child costs more, you generally have higher levels of debt and have more 'doodads' to service.

So how do you break out of the trap you are in? How do you liberate some money to start investing in assets that will generate a largely passive income? You need to add another job title to that which you have already. You need to become a 'Freedom Fighter' for your money.

Part of the Freedom Fighter's job description is to find ways to liberate small amounts of cash from Sainsbury's, from Threshers, from B&Q and from Costa Coffee. But how can you know how much you can liberate if you don't know what you put into captivity in the first place?

Get fighting, freedom fighters!

ACTION STEP

Do you feel at all motivated now to get out your envelopes of receipts and the file of neatly filed bank and credit card statements yet?

How about a guerrilla attack on just totting up some rough monthly outgoings?

Pay It Forward First

Have you seen that great film 'Pay It Forward'?

A little boy is set a project by his teacher to come up with an idea that will change the world. He struggles and struggles but then comes up with the idea that if just three people committed random acts of kindness for three other people and then, instead of expecting a 'payback', asked those three people to do the same for three more people, it would change the world.

And in a quantum leap from geometry to algebra...

*'What I learned from the experience (college chemistry)
is that it doesn't always matter if you understand
the details. As long as you get the formula right,
you can count on the results.'*

Mary Hunt, 'Debt Proof Living'

In her great book, Mary Hunt talks about the formula for debt proof living as being 10–10–80 and this is how it works. For every pound that flows into your life, you should give away 10%, save/invest 10% and live on 80%.

Yeah, right! I can hear you say, 'I can't afford to give anything away,' and I would have to say that even a little while ago I would have been right there with you.

But she makes a compelling argument for giving or tithing before you even start to earn, and some of the things she says in the book struck home with me and lodged there.

Two of the reasons that I found compelling were:

1. It has to do with balance (there are those scales again!). When you give to others first and then care enough about yourself, your family and your future to say that some is yours to keep (10% saving/investing), then your insatiable desires are 'hushed up'.

2. Giving teaches your brain that you have more than enough. You see things differently and your vision changes. I believe that giving helps you believe in the financial abundance all around. When you give, you are telling yourself that you are beyond scarcity, and you are being grateful in advance.

If you have never been a giver, facing the 10% hurdle can be daunting. If this is the case, start with 1% or 2%. But get into the habit, do it 30 times. And then increase it slowly.

Remember, you don't have to know how it works, just that it does. And it doesn't have to be money – it can be time or skills, but it seems to work better with money. Every time I give away wealth coaching in some form, I attract new clients at full rate. Works every time.

ACTION STEP

Who will you pay it forward to?

Pick a charity or good cause right now and resolve to find out how to easily and painlessly make donations. Perhaps you can pay by automated debit online every time you receive a salary or other kind of cheque. Make it simple – don't get bogged down in all that 'covenant' stuff for a while, just give. You can get more sophisticated as you get the habit. Even if you just work out how much a week you will give and then drop it into a Big Issue seller's hat (if homeless people are your 'thing').

Side Note: The Big Issue (*www.BigIssue.co.uk)* has become the Money Gym's official charity because they help the homeless to help themselves. It's a two way street with the vendors having to prove they are trying to help themselves first in terms of overcoming their various addictions, and they have to agree to behave a certain way in public when selling the newspaper retail (that they have bought wholesale).

In March 2009 we handed over a cheque for £4500 which we raised from our Property Extravaganza day and it was one of the proudest moments of my life so far. The room was full of experienced and aspiring property investors all of whom were there because they had read this book or experienced one of our wealth creation programmes... Something I could never have envisaged when I first wrote the eprogramme that turned into this book, back in 2003.

I also really enjoy donating to Kiva because what you donate, they lend to micro-businesses around the world on your behalf, and you choose who you want to lend to, and then you re-lend again when the micro loans are paid back. You can join the Money Gym team at *www.kiva.org/team/themoneygym*

Pay Yourself First

When I read Robert Kiyosaki's 'Rich Dad, Poor Dad' I was struck with the (new to me!) concept that you should ensure that you pay yourself first, before the tax man, the supermarket, the garage round the corner, that little Italian restaurant you like to visit.

It turned on its head the concept that you deserve a treat occasionally and that you could cheer yourself up with a frothy cappuccino because it didn't cost very much and made you feel better about your overdraft somehow.

Have you ever wondered why – sometimes – poor people have such great cars outside the houses that they don't own? Drive round any council estate in the UK and you will see that it's true. Where do you think the term 'ghetto fabulous' came from? Who are those people paying first?

I had always thought that you should pay the most you can, to everyone you owe, regardless of whether you can afford it or not. Somehow, that seemed to be more 'in integrity' to me. But who did that serve? Certainly not me.

Was it a self esteem issue, I wonder, this notion that everyone was more deserving of my money than me?

What Is This Paying Yourself First Business Exactly?

We have just talked about 'Paying It Forward First' and I should be clear that Paying Yourself First comes *after* Paying it Forward First.

And then when we talk about paying yourself first, it should be clear that when you pay yourself first, you buy assets with the proceeds, not 'doodads'! When you buy 'doodads', you are just paying the supplier of that 'doodad' before you, your family and your future.

Who do you pay first at the moment? Who are you allowing to hold your money prisoner?

This is another scary concept for folks struggling to make ends meet. The idea is to pay yourself first 10% of every pound or dollar you earn. If your finances are super–tight every month, then start with your net take home and work up to your gross income before tax, otherwise you are still paying the tax man before you.

And what will you do with the 10% of net or gross income you are paying yourself first with? For the time being, just stick it somewhere safe, where you can get at while earning a little interest. We'll cover the practicalities in Chapter 3 – Cashflow.

Your Comfort Zone

I saw a big article in the paper a while ago about how many intelligent, articulate people are getting phobic about money. Symptoms include racing heart, feelings of depression, avoidance of all money pages, programmes and the business section of the news. They don't open bank statements and they totally disconnect from thinking that what they spend today will turn up on a credit card or overdraft statement tomorrow.

The cause of this new phobia is quite simply overwhelm. They can't cope with the information overload about life insurance, term assurance, income replacement policies, Tessas, ISAs, flexible mortgages, endowment policies and the many other mortgages, so they simply switch off. Especially if they have been miss–sold a product or they have invested hard earned cash into savings vehicles that have lost value!

People simply do not know what to do, or where to turn, for the best. They don't trust advisors (sorry! but it's true!) and so they just give up. They decide to live now because it seems nothing they do can make it any better.

This book is all about taking it back to the basics. Keeping it simple. I could bombard you with the technical stuff but I know that you are probably in overwhelm already and – if you could cope then you probably wouldn't have bought this book!

And it's not your fault that you are in overwhelm because it's not in anyone's interest to keep it simple. The financial services industry, in their eagerness to offer a product for everyone, are only trying to help (while making a buck admittedly, but we know that's not a crime, don't we?)

So what I do is get you to look at, and think about, all the emotional and historical reasons you are where you are with your money. I ask you to consider how it would feel to get on top of it and really feel in control.

And then, very slowly, I ask you to take one step at a time out of that locked–down box where you and your finances might have been living for a while now. Just start keeping the receipts. Just get the paperwork sorted out, which in itself will probably make you feel better.

My hope is that, by Module 3, with my support, you are feeling able to tackle some slightly more uncomfortable stuff.

So that you are able to start to move 'out of the red and into the rich'.

ACTION STEP

If you haven't done any of the exercises yet, if you haven't started keeping your receipts, if you haven't sorted out your paperwork into the files, then now is the time to do it. We are moving from the soft, fluffy, woolly part of the book into the practical, action orientated part and you won't be ready unless you start to take some action.

Trust me, do the prep and we'll start to move forward together. Are you ready?

Fake It Till You Make It

What makes you look and feel wealthy? Gill Fielding used to start her wealth creation seminars by asking people why they believed that she was qualified to teach them about becoming wealthy. The answers were always really interesting.

- 'Because I have heard you are a millionaire.'

- 'Because you live in a big house.'

- 'Because you spend time looking after yourself – always at the gym, pool, masseuse etc.'

- 'Because you don't have to work?'

- 'Because you are immaculately groomed.'

- 'Because you used to be an Accountant.'

- 'Because you say so.'

All of these answers are subjective and none prove that Gill was qualified to talk about wealth. In fact she used to say that being an Accountant had been a distinct disadvantage when it came to making money! But everyone had paid to be there in her seminars or weekends, so something about Gill had made them trust her skills and her knowledge. They believed that she could teach it (whatever *it* was) to them.

What makes you think that I can teach you about wealth creation? Is it the hotel? The fact that I say so? Is it the newsletter? It can't be the pictures! I'm too casual to be rich – surely. What made you trust me enough to spend some money, and just as importantly, time to find out what I've got to say?

When I looked at this question, I realised that it was the fingernails for me. Anyone who could spend that much time (or money if you are paying a manicurist!) doing their nails, had to be wealthy. And if Gill had made it herself, then she could show me how. Then I looked a bit closer at what wealth meant for me, personally.

My vision of wealth involves me living in an old house, beautifully decorated in light, warm colours, surrounded by dark wood antiques listening to classical music. It is clean and very, very tidy. My hair is nice, my nails are immaculate, my clothes are ironed. I work because I love it but I don't have to go anywhere particularly unless I travel business class and stay in nice hotels. I can pick the kids up from school but I don't have to do the housework. There is always enough of everything – I never run out of food, toiletries, makeup. I have bubbles in my bath every time. I don't rush.

It's interesting how many elements in there have nothing to do with actually being wealthy. And interestingly, I was almost punishing myself for not being more successful, by being too frugal with stuff like bubble bath.

So here's how I fake it, till I make it.

I listen to classical music in the car. I buy two of everything until I always have a reserve of one in the cupboard. I have re–arranged my day so that I don't have appointments after 3pm and make sure I have time to get everywhere without rushing. I insist on things being tidy around me and previously I loved moving into the hotel so that my wonderful cleaner looked after my surroundings. I now still have a cleaner as she does a better job than I ever could.

I say 'no' to speaking engagements unless I travel comfortably and easily in the middle of the day. I like to stay overnight so that I don't end up driving, miserable and alone, for hours on end, late at night.

And do you know something? It worked. I felt wealthier immediately.

So how could you fake it till you make it?

Imagine yourself, ten years on, and you have made it. What specifically are you enjoying about being wealthy?

What little treats do you enjoy that you didn't before?

How could you *now*, at little extra cost, make yourself feel wealthy and worth it?

Beware The Financial Boogieman!

So many self–employed people spend so much time and energy trying to find ways of not paying tax that they forget to do the important thing – make money. I often hear people saying things like, 'oh you don't want to be self employed or make more money because you end having to deal with all that paperwork or end up paying it all in tax'.

What people forget is that you only have to pay tax if you *make a profit*. And you only have to pay tax on a percentage of your profit. And you have tax allowances on the money you make, before they even calculate your tax. If you have a company, then it has its own tax allowance; it is counted as a physical entity separate from you.

Even if you end up having to pay tax at the dreaded 40-50%, what does that actually mean? That you are keeping 50-60% of your profits. And profit means total income less legitimate expenses.

If you are employed, you might have to pay for your own mobile phone, magazines and training seminars. These have to be paid out of your after–tax income. If you have a business on the side of your day job, you can claim many of those things as allowable business expenses so you get the benefit before you ever have to pay any tax.

Interesting? We will cover this in more detail in the Mind Your Own Business Module but suffice to say that making lots of money is good, having as many legitimate expenses as possible is good, one of which is your tax specialist and accountancy bill, paying even 40% tax is good because you are keeping 60% of the extra money – extra money is good. The independence that comes from earning your own money separately from your day job is very good.

Similarly, so many self–employed people end up in trouble with the tax man because they won't spend a little bit of time and money to get good tax advice from a specialist accountant. They are scared of incurring lots of terrible charges.

Let me tell you, the tax bills you may end up incurring would be a lot more terrible, if you ignore this advice. But we are coming full circle here now.

Be wary! The taxman can be your friend if you keep good records and have a good tax advisor and/or accountant. But possibly the real boogieman is the worst kind of accountant – one who is complacent and who does not do what they are supposed to do.

One of my clients had an accountant that charged her over £300 to reply to her telephone query asking a question that basically required a 'yes' or 'no' answer. So she was understandably reluctant to call him again. At the end of the year, she received the usual bill and assumed, as you would, that this was for checking the books that had been prepared by her book–keeper. But no, it was just for signing off on those books – not checking or querying them, not looking them over to see where she can make tax savings. And now she has a larger tax bill than anticipated plus a routine tax audit and will have to pay the expensive accountant even more money to oversee the audit. The words 'salt' and 'wound' come to mind.

How would you know that some accountants are more pro–active than others unless you know a few? How would you know that some specialise in tax, some in retrospective or historical accounts and some in being pro–active. You wouldn't. You can go on recommendation but there are as many accountants as there are solicitors (or coaches!)

My client is now in talks with a more pro–active accountant who will be paid on a monthly retainer basis, to avoid nasty shocks in the future, both with the bill and the tax due. He is completely reviewing how her businesses are set up so that they are as tax efficient as possible.

Who's the real financial boogieman? The tax office or complacent accountants?

ACTION STEP

Have a beauty parade! Make an appointment with three accountants, for a complementary introductory session. Tell them about your personal circumstances and your aspirations. Then let them tell you how they can help you. How their firm can support you in making money and saving tax. Ask them if they are investors themselves.

You will soon get a feel for the good ones. And if you are not sure, make appointments with three more. You'll learn a lot in the process.

How To Mindfeed

What is the greatest asset you can have? What will enable you to pick yourself up, dust yourself off and start again, even if you lose everything?

Property tycoon, Russ Whitney, used to send off for every wealth creation scheme he saw advertised until finally he bought a tiny book that gave him the knowledge that he needed to be able to make money from property. He has gone on to create a multi–million training company teaching people how to make money from property.

I was an under–achiever at school. Far too boring. But luckily my mother instilled a love of reading into me at a very young age. And in addition to romantic historical novels and science fiction, I used to buy every 'How To' self help book on the market without even knowing that they were called self help books. 'How To Make Great Decisions', 'How To Love A Difficult Man' and 'How To Become A Woman of Substance' were three of the early ones.

My friends used to tease me mercilessly and I used to have to hide the books in a cupboard; but I couldn't quite throw them away. I didn't know it, but I was searching for the education I didn't get at school.

Why couldn't I throw them away when read? Because I felt instinctively that somewhere in those books was The Secret. Now I'm not talking about the famous film of the same name which came out after this book was written.

The Secret was the one magical thing that would make me successful. The key. The power. What I didn't realise, as I bought and read the books, but often didn't do all the exercises (oh, no, far too simple and obvious) was that it was not *one* thing that would make the difference.

What was I missing? The fact that it's not one idea, not one secret, not even any one exercise, but a process. A process of education; of resisting the negativity that we are surrounded with day by day. It's a layering upon layering of ideas and ways of thinking, of glimmers of possibility, of keeping one's motivation going, of not giving up.

In the same way that fairy stories never quite fade from one's memory, making it exciting – even as a cynical 40 year old – to go into some sun speckled, dew drenched woods in early morning (you never quite know if you *may* see a fairy toadstool ring and hear laughter as the dancers flee), by continually exposing yourself to educational and 'How To' books and seminars, particularly around money and wealth creation, you are feeding your mind.

Mike Litman, author of 'Conversations With Millionaires', says that one of the best reasons to set a goal to become a millionaire is for what you will learn along the way.

And if you learn something new, just one thing perhaps from each book, you are growing an asset so powerful, so creative, so full of potential for wealth creation, that one day you will explode with an idea that will create more abundance than you can even imagine now.

ACTION STEP

Go to your bookshelf and dig out any books on wealth creation you have ever bought and all the folders from the seminars you've attended. Dust them off and start reading them again (and if you haven't bought any yet, get started with 'Rich Dad, Poor Dad' by Robert Kiyosaki).

This time, do the exercises suggested at the end of each chapter, if there are any. See what works for you. And by 'works', I don't mean makes loads of money spontaneously appear in your bank account. I mean, see what tweaks your thinking, gets your creativity flowing, keeps your motivation high. I actually use reading as a form of meditation – even if you read a book twice you pick up new stuff each time, I find.

Your Greatest Gift

Following on from talking about your greatest asset – your mind, I would like move onto another great asset you have. You. Your soul if you like, your spirit, the essence of you. While your mind will enable you to pick yourself up, dust yourself off and start again, even if you lose everything, it is your spirit, your soul, your you–ness will make you want to do so.

At school we all pick up that we should fit in and not stand out from the crowd, to be normal. It's a very powerful cultural force. In stone-age days it was a protective mechanism but nowadays it is very limiting and, if you are serious about becoming financially abundant, being normal is positively dangerous. Many of my clients experience great resistance and negativity when they start to work with me – often from the people that love them the most – parents, spouses, siblings, best friends. Often it is people who are better off than you (but who don't know how they did it!) that will caution you the loudest. You will need to be strong to overcome that wall of negativity that will rise up in front of you.

I used to work in the music industry and it is popularly assumed that you must be a shark in order to succeed. So everyone was busy being sharks and double–crossing each other every way you turned. But when I really looked about me I saw that the really successful and admired people were the ones with integrity. The managers who were still looking after their successful acts twenty years on, with no more than a handshake.

When I attended Dave Buck's seminar at the Coachville Conference in Las Vegas 2002, he planted the seed that, in order to become truly, wildly successful, the more 'YOU' you can become, the more you will attract people to you, who can and will want to help you on your road to riches. Building on that, with the following quote by Marianne Williamson (popularly attributed to Nelson Mandela!) has set me free to be as great as I know I can be:

'We ask ourselves, who am I to be brilliant, gorgeous, talented, fabulous? Actually who are you NOT to be?'

Recommended Reading
- 'Think & Grow Rich' – Napoleon Hill
- 'You Were Born Rich' – Bob Procter
- 'Richest Man In Babylon' – George S Clason
- 'Conversations With Millionaires' – Mike Litman & Jason Oman

THE MONEY GYM WORKOUT PLAN

These are the actions I will take in the next month, arising from
Module 2: Beliefs, Behaviours & Attitudes

1. _____

2. _____

3. _____

4. _____

5. _____

6. _____

7. _____

8. _____

9. _____

10. _____

11. _____

12. _____

13. _____

14. _____

15. _____

16. _____

17. _____

18. _____

19. _____

20. _____

Signed: _____ Date: _____

CHAPTER 3
Cash Flow

The Different Kinds of Cash Flows

This is where we start getting into the nitty gritty, so if you haven't done all the exercises from Modules 1 and 2 you may want to go back now and do them now.

If you have read 'Rich Dad, Poor Dad' by Robert Kiyosaki, then you'll know that there are three kinds of income flows. As an aside, it really does help if we use the water analogy with money because it gives us a sense that money flows through, in and out of your life, it's not static – although to employed people, looking at a pay check that never grows, it may well feel pretty static.

There is earned income flow, passive income flow and portfolio income flow.

We know about earned income, that's when we have to show up, do something, perform to a pre–arranged standard, stay somewhere until someone else says we can go home, where we have no control over the security of our jobs. But it's an essential income flow, especially in the early days of building our wealth, so it's best to try and earn as much as possible, while working somewhere where we can gain some skills, experience or contacts, that will help us in later life.

The interesting thing is, that most people don't imagine that they can have additional income flows if they have earned income. The thought of starting a business part time, or doing some network marketing for a product they love, or developing some intellectual property from something they know or are passionate about... this just does not cross their mind.

'I work too hard, I'm too tired,' they say. At the risk of becoming very unpopular here – rubbish! There is a lot of dead time in anyone's day, time in the car, time on the train (commuting, while tiring, is great for this), time in the evenings, time at weekends. It's almost as if the action of earning a living lets them off the hook for taking responsibility for their own financial lives. Must be something to do with the employee mindset perhaps, but the good news is that you can grow out of it. The other difference is that when you are developing something for yourself, your energy levels rise dramatically!

People always say to me, 'I don't know how you do it all,' and yes, I know I do work harder than most, possibly too hard, but what people forget is that I enjoy what I do – actually I love it! So the line between work and fun/leisure blurs. Would I rather watch rubbish on TV or write my newsletter?

Easy, every time. Except for X=Factor, Jamie O, Gordon Ramsey, The Apprentice, any property programme and any forensic pathology thing obviously!

These people always imagine that they have to spend all of their spare time doing the 'other activity'. Not so. Just one hour a day will move you forward and in one year, you may have a very respectable other income. Colin Turner's book 'Swimming With Piranhas Makes You Hungry' is great for helping you clear out the clutter in your life to make room for other activities and it is very motivational too.

Actually, that's a common belief among people who are just starting out on their financial journey – that to do something well, you have to spend all your time doing it – that 'all or nothing' mentality. I notice it in myself a lot. And it manifests itself in taking no action at all. But in my experience, any action or even a little bit of action taken regularly, makes a world of difference. If you just change 1% every day, that's a complete u-turn in less than half a year.

But this is still earned activity. The next income flow you may experience is Portfolio Income. This is where you receive income from your portfolio of investments. Investments in the stockmarket, investments in businesses or investments in property. You may already own some shares and receive dividends from those shares. They probably get paid right back to the company to increase your shareholding, but it's still dividend portfolio income. Some people have so many shares they live on the income from the dividends.

I would count rent from buy-to-let and a salary/dividend from a family owned firm as portfolio income. Downline income from network marketing is portfolio income. In fact, anything where you have to invest a modicum of time, effort or knowledge is portfolio income.

And the final type of income, the Holy Grail of Financial Intelligence, is Passive Income. True passive income can grow out of Earned Income and Portfolio Income, for example where you have so many buy to let flats that you hire a property agent or manager to look after them for you. You just turn up once a quarter, every six months or once a year to review the figures.

This book generates passive income. It grew out of earned income (the programme I use with my one–to–one clients)!

My old music industry website ArtistManager was largely passive income as it made me money without my having to do anything on a day to day basis. I used to think about it, and email my software designer with ideas for improving it, but that's pretty much all. It earned up to £200 in a week in its heyday. Other passive income sources include book royalties, licensing fees from artwork, for greetings cards, scarf & wallpaper manufacture etc, and if you write a top selling hit song you are made for life.

How many people know that Dolly Parton made more money from the song 'I Will Always Love You' than Whitney Houston did? And Dolly didn't have to get out of bed once she had written it. Now that's a nice thought, isn't it?

ACTION STEP

What can you do or what do you know about, that could be turned into earned income, then portfolio income, then passive income? Pick something you are interested in or passionate about, then it won't seem like work. We go into this in more detail in a later module 'Profit From Your Passion' but you can get thinking now.

Allocate half an hour a day (and yes you do have time), just to think about it, and then when you have The Idea (and you will) you'll already have half an hour free to take some action on it.

The Financial Integrity Model

'Most people put their wants before their needs, and their needs before their integrity, when it comes to their finances. 'I want a new car' or 'I would love to be free' comes first, then 'I need to earn more money' or for some people, 'I need to be free' but they never think about their financial integrity. Freedom is not a want or a need, but a luxury, a luxury that comes from financial integrity, a luxury that must be earned.'

Paraphrased from the Personal Foundation – Finances tape by Thomas Leonard

I was working with Gill Fielding, my then wealth mentor, when my personal coach Rachel Turner, sent me the Financial segment of Thomas' Personal Foundation audiotapes. The above sentence really struck me and provided the missing piece of the jigsaw. Thank you Thomas!

This is a short sharp shock day. Brace yourselves.

Many people leave their day job without knowing how they are going to support themselves and, I have to say, new coaches are the worst for this. They hear all the talk about abundance and the 'universe providing' and think that somehow, even with no marketing skills, no niche and no reservoir of potential clients, that people will be beating their door down to give them money.

Perhaps they have a redundancy payment, or some savings, and think that the deadline of their money running out in three months will force them to take action and create a successful new business from scratch.

Well, it ain't gonna happen. How can you have 'Cashflow' if no cash is flowing?

I regularly experience new clients coming to me for Financial Intelligence Coaching and the first thing we have to talk about is how they are going to pay their mortgage at the end of the month. Magic wand time again.

The first thing I have to tell them is that I can help them work miracles on their business, *but* it will take a minimum of three months to build enough momentum even if they work at it flat out (by which I mean 5–10 hours a week) where currently they often only have time in their lives to come to a one hour call!

They say that they have to leave their job because they don't have time to apply themselves to their new business unless they do. Then they leave, and their time gets filled up with putting the washing on, having lunch with friends, doing all the self–care things that they have always wanted to do and spending time with the kids.

Let me tell you now, building any new business can be a full time job – or at least it requires the equivalent of full time dedication, even if out of office hours.

Before leaving any job, you need to ensure that you can pay at least the basic bills for a good long time, six months to a year minimum, and then that you can afford to hire a mentor who has built a successful business in a short period of time, using the methods you think you will feel comfortable with.

Otherwise how are you going to know what to do, that works?

And unless you are in 'Financial Integrity' you will not be able to start any of the forthcoming steps to create financial freedom. Financial Integrity is defined as having more money coming in than is going out.

Is Your Cashflow In Integrity?
The Pyramid of Financial Power

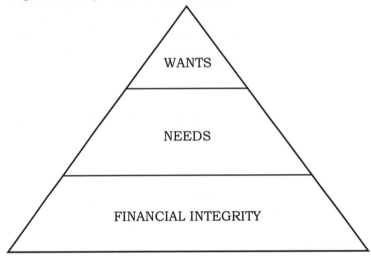

'Annual income twenty pounds, annual expenditure nineteen pounds, nineteen shillings and sixpence, result happiness. Annual income twenty pounds, annual expenditure twenty pounds ought and six, result misery.'

Mr Micawber, in David Copperfield: Dickens

Or to put it another way...

Annual income £20.00 + annual expenditure £19.50 = Financial Integrity

Annual income £20.00 + annual expenditure £20.50 = No Financial Integrity

So the importance of the Cashflow module to you is...

Before you can go on to learn about the best ways to use your money to build financial freedom, you have to find ways to reduce your outgoings *or* increase your income flows in order to create the 'spare cash' that you can put to work for you, building your Pyramid of Financial Power.

ACTION STEP

1. If you are working and thinking of leaving your job, join The Money Gym for your 30 day free trial, and download a copy of Mike Neill's 'Freedom Fund' article from our website and put it into action. Mike's a great coach.

2. If you have already left work, find out how much money you have now, and how many months it will last you. That's how long you have left to make it work.

3. If you have no money, and don't know how to pay the bills at the end of the month, get a job, sell something or at the very worst, get a loan. It won't be forever, but you have to have money coming in, no matter how little, or be able to pay your bills for 3–6 months to be able to build your business. You will then be able to move forward.

Wealth Building Exercise: Monthly Income / Outgoings List (Budget)

For some people, this will be the first time they have sat down and really listed all their income and outgoings. Most of the time, as long as they have enough to cover their bills each month, they don't examine things any more closely.

This attitude is more common than you may think. A very shrewd business owner friend of mine told me the other day that she doesn't have monthly management accounts, her staff could be ripping her off and she wouldn't know. As long as the bank balance is roughly the same at the end of each month, she doesn't worry. And then she wonders why she doesn't make much of a profit.

Becoming wealthy is not about how much money you earn, it's about how much of that money you keep. And the first step to working out how to keep more of it, is knowing about cashflow. What cash flows in, and what flows out?

The closer you can stick to these categories the easier it will be to use the simple cashflow forecast spreadsheet that you will use when you have gathered all of the information together. You can get a link to the spreadsheet when you join The Money Gym Silver Level on a 30 day free trial.

INCOME	
Net Salary 1	
Net salary 2	
Interest	
Dividends	
Other	
Other	
Total Income	
EXPENSES	
Personal spending	
Capital, repairs etc	
Children	
Taxes	
Holidays	
Food	
Travel	
Phone and gas	
TV license	
Car repairs	
Businesses	
Credit card repayments	
Entertaining & leisure	
Standing Orders	
Direct Debits	
Other	
Total Expenses	
Net Income	

Setting Your 'Rack Rate'

I had an amazing client called Sally. She was a high powered, dynamic person who solves other people's problems, working particularly with fast growing companies whose turnover is growing faster than their ability to recruit staff. With a house in the country, a flat in Fulham and a very fancy car, you would think she had it made. But no, Sally is stressed, always fire–fighting financially and struggles to pay her bills at the end of the month. She often ends up undercharging to get clients, over–working and feeling deeply resentful.

Another client is a holistic therapist who works wonders with aromatherapy massage. If you have a bad back, have emotional blocks, are stuck in your life or just want to treat yourself, Fiona is the person to see. Everyone sings her praises but she is not yet making a truly great living from what she does. Why not?

Yet another client is Hermione, who works in the city for a big bank. She is an employee and every month she stares in despair at her salary cheque – she is paid well, but it doesn't feel like enough for what she has to do and it certainly doesn't go as far as she wants it to – which is a holiday home in France!

The problem is the same for all. They haven't grasped that they will never earn what they want unless they get very specific about what they want to earn.

I have to thank my then business coach Chris Barrow for this module.

Chris, at the time, worked with two kinds of clients; firstly in the UK with dentists and worldwide with coaches via the Million Dollar Coaching Practice. And it was in one of his workshops that I really 'got' the message about setting your fees or hourly rate based not on what you earn now, but what you want to earn, also thinking about how long in terms of days and hours you want to work.

The magical thing about setting your 'rack–rate' even if you are employed and earning much less than you want, is that it really focuses your mind on the fact that your standard of living is not going to improve unless you *do* something about it.

Even more magically, it somehow makes you feel worth your new hourly rate and gets you focused on what you want to be earning. If it turns out that your actual hourly rate is much less than your ideal 'rack rate' you can tell yourself that you are simply 'discounting' temporarily.

Many of my clients have gone on to improve themselves in order to qualify for promotions, some have immediately applied for better paid jobs, or created other income streams in order to come up to their 'rack rate' more quickly. Most have stopped diddling about and got serious, very fast.

How serious can you get about creating the income stream you deserve?

ACTION STEP

You can download a tipsheet on how to set your 'rack–rate' at my website TheMoneyGym.com I would also recommend again the book 'Swimming With Piranha Makes You Hungry' by Colin Turner. It may be out of print now because you can't buy it new at Amazon, but you will be able to get a new copy in bookshops or a second hand copy via Amazon.

Your Bath Runneth Over

The last thing anyone wants in real life is an overflowing bath – it can be one of the more expensive domestic disasters!

But when thinking of all the wealth in the world as the Sea of Abundance, if you can imagine that you are entitled to at least a bath full of Abundance for yourself, you can get a great mental picture going.

Your various income flows are the ways that you fill up the bath. Some incomes will be like filling it up with a teaspoon or a teacup, some will be like filling it with buckets. You could turn the taps and the shower on, you could run a hosepipe in. The more ways you fill your Bath of Abundance, the quicker you will get to the place where you hardly have to do anything, and it spills over on a regular basis, effortlessly. That is when you can have some fun, dancing and sploshing in the puddles you make (or spending the excess income, if you like!)

BUT... beware, because your bath can have more than one plughole. All the time you are working – both creatively and in the usual ways – to fill it up, there can be more and more plugholes mysteriously appearing. What are these plugholes? Standing orders and direct debits.

I used to find it very easy to spend on something as long as I was paying monthly and not having to fork out in one lump sum. So I accumulated so many plugholes it was unbelievable! As fast as I tried to fill my bath, the faster the money ran away. And I had to earn more and more just to keep the water level steady... let alone make it rise to the magical brimming overflow level.

There is something very disempowering about having lots of standing orders and direct debits coming out of your bank account every month, all on different days, never when you expect. It's even worse for self–employed people whose income may not come in exactly on the 1st of the month.

Direct debits particularly seem to me like one sure way to hand over control of your bank account to someone else.

One of the turning points for me came when I started to look at all of my direct debits and standing orders as extra plugholes in my bath. When considering a new purchase, I would think, yes, I could afford it on a monthly basis but do I really want it, knowing that it would make it even harder to fill my bath to overflowing? Could I pay in one hit, rather that monthly?

WEALTH WARNING!

It is particularly easy to sign up online for that essential new bit of software or service, via your credit card, then very hard to cancel that subscription! If you are involved in online businesses, one way to overcome that is to either using a pay as you go card or have one card for each business and use it only for online purchases and direct debits on that business. Then, if you want to start fresh you just pay off, then cancel that card.

Your Bath of Wealth

Imagine each hole as being one of your existing standing orders or direct debits. Who among us does not have a bath like this?

ACTION STEP

How can you speed up the time when your Bath of Abundance overflows?

First of all, get a printout of all your current standing orders and direct debits.

Look at each one – do you really need them all or are there out of date payments on there, for things you no longer use. Cancel the ones you really don't need any more.

Look at your credit card statements and try to do the same. If you can't work out how to cancel any regular payments via the vendor's website, transfer the balance to a new, lower interest rate, card, and cancel the old card.

Before setting up any other payments, think to yourself 'This is another plughole in my Bath of Abundance – do I really need it or could I pay in one hit?'

In An Ideal World...

One of the first steps to setting some real, measurable targets for wealth creation is to work out where you would like your income to come from. Don't get hung up on reality here, let's just play for a while.

Let's look at your **earned income**. If you won the lottery, would you still work at anything? What would it be? Are you doing it now? How would it change? How much of your total income do you want your earned income to be? 30 percent? 50 percent? Or perhaps just 10 percent.

My hotel was earned income for a while at the beginning because I had to be there, for it to work properly.

Portfolio income is income that you don't have to turn up at an office every day to earn, or don't have to be actually present all day every day to create But it does require some input from you on a fairly regular basis. How much of total projected income flow would you like to be generated from this kind of income? 50 percent? 80? 30?

With the hotel, as soon as I recruited a manager, trained and managed them, with daily calls, weekly focus sessions and monthly management meetings, while I kept an eye on the Business Dashboard Indicators (more about this in the Mind Your Own Business module), then it would turn into part of my portfolio income. I am able to do more than one thing at a time, and continue to build a portfolio of things, including my coaching, e–commerce income, artistmanager.com, investing in property and shares/equities.

What about **passive income?** This is income that you don't do anything to maintain, beyond an hour or two every so often. What kind of passive income would you like? A fully automated internet business? Book royalties? E–programme income? Perhaps you would like to paint and have your paintings turned into greetings cards? Property income only counts as passive income if you intend to have a lettings agent manage it for you. Equity investing only counts as passive income if you are buying shares that yield a dividend and require the minimum of input from you.

As soon as I recruited a manager to live in at the hotel, and run the place for me, then it became largely passive income. I involved him in the business and gave him a profit related bonus, so he was as keen for it to do well as I was and as careful about costs, so it could have become very passive income.

You can see how this can work very powerfully. Imagine one of your passive income segments was 'book royalties'. Even if you have no idea yet of the kind of book you want to write, you can see that if you put down your intention to earn £10,000 per year from book royalties, you have moved one or two steps closer to realising that intention. Each journey is made up of a thousand steps and you just have to take the first one or two to get started.

Beware of trying to do be 'realistic' when doing this exercise. Do it as if I had a magic wand (Oops! There it is again!) and could make it all come true for you. 'Realistic' kills dreams, squashes inspiration, makes life less of an adventure. 'Realistic' is the worst enemy of those first few steps. Trust your subconscious – if you put down in black and white how you want your money to flow, but haven't got a clue how to go about it, then your subconscious will get beavering away on a solution.

ACTION STEP

Draw a large circle on a piece of paper, and divide it into three segments, earned, passive and portfolio income.

Now look at each one and divide it up into the kinds of earned, portfolio and passive income you would like to cultivate. Only have three mini–segments for each. Remember, this is not set in tablets of stone; you can always change or replace any segment later. Put the percentages in, for example, perhaps you have 50% of your income being passive, and let's imagine you have chosen 'book royalties' as one of your mini–segments.

So, let's get even more specific.

If you want to earn £100,000 per annum, with 50% being passive, and 20% of that coming from book royalties, that means you need to earn £10,000 per annum from some sort of book deal. That can either be advances on one book per year of £10,000, or an advance every other year of £20,000, or no publishing advances at all, but you could sell via the internet, say 10 ebooks a week at £19.20 or 20 per week at £9.61.

You could now create a mindmap for each income flow and break down each one into different actions to take, investigations to make, people to talk to, websites to visit, books to read.

Finish your chart and finally, pin it up somewhere you can see it every day. Let that old subconscious get to work.

The Money Filter

One of the most powerful tools the wealthy have at their disposal is a Money Filter. It enables them to legally filter more of their money into their pocket, before the tax man takes his share.

How Does This Money Filter Work?

Imagine you earn £1000 per month. Usually you would get taxed on that £1000 after taking into account your tax allowance. Say that you are taxed at 25%, so you end up with £750 after tax. Then you have to pay for your car and your mobile phone, together totalling £200 per month. That would leave you with £550 per month.

Now imagine you have your Money Filter in place. It changes things around completely.

You earn your £1000, pay for your mobile phone and car, £200 as before, then you get taxed 25% on the £800 left. Deduction of £200, you have filtered £50 into your pocket.

Too Good To Be Legal?

Wait, it gets better. Imagine that you have a day job, and you have paid the £250 tax. If you have a Money Filter running alongside your day job, you can use it to pay for many of the things that you use every day, but don't get tax allowances for, in your day job.

For example, one of my Money Filters allows me to buy music magazines, buy tickets for and attend award ceremonies at the Hilton (with accommodation), buy CD's and DVD's, and travel all over the world, to Miami and the South of France in particular.

If my Money Filter spends slightly more than it earns, then I can even claim some of the £250 back out of the tax I paid from my day job.

What is this Money Filter? It's simply a little business on the side of your day job, a sole tradership or a partnership.

There is an even more sophisticated Money Filter available. It almost doubles the amount you are allowed to earn before you pay any tax. It is called a Limited Company. Each Limited Company has its own tax allowance, so the expenses (mobile phone, car) come off the earnings first, then the allowance is applied to the profits, then the taxman takes his cut.

And an even more sophisticated version exists. That is where the entity who owns the Limited Company is another company, based in a country where there are no taxes payable at all. That company can be wholly owned by a person living in this country.

These money filters effectively send the taxman from the front of the queue with his hand out for your money, to the back of the queue, after the mobile phone company and the car company, allowing you to enjoy the gadgets and gizmos out of pre–taxed income, rather than post–taxed income.

ACTION STEP

Are you starting to think that it might be worth turning the telly off one evening a week and starting a little second business? Is the motivation growing in you yet? Would you like to run your phone or your car (or even a better version of either) out of the money that you usually pay the tax man?

Important Disclaimer: I must add here that you should ALWAYS seek the advice of an accountant as to what is allowable against tax in any kind of business. My marketing jaunts to the Winter Music Conference in Miami Beach would not have been allowable if your second business was selling knitted loo roll covers for example! I can't claim clothes against tax but my sister, an opera singer, can claim stage outfits. The tax man is not stupid, after all.

Eat Me -v- Feed Me

When you first get interested in Wealth Creation one of the first questions is 'so how do I find these opportunities'?

A little bit later, you will find that you are overwhelmed with all the possibilities and opportunities are jumping out at you from every corner. So how can you tell which ones to pursue?

If you have read Rich Dad, Poor Dad by Robert Kiyosaki, you will know about the 'Does it Eat Me, or does it Feed Me?' question and it's a really useful first yardstick of how good a deal may be.

Does it put money in your pocket or take money out of your pocket? If you have to invest some money to get to the opportunity, how much, for how long, and what will your return on that investment be by the end of the first year? This is known as your Return On Investment or ROI.

If you can see that something will be putting money into your pocket within a year, and there is another deal that won't, which one will you go for?

If you can see that one deal will return you 10% within a year, and one will return 30%, which deal is the more attractive?

What about one deal where the return will be 30% but will take you longer than one year, and be harder work, against a deal that will return 20% but start returning in six months and is safer?

This is where many new investors and entrepreneurs come unstuck. They don't work out their strategy and stick to it; so they alternate between fear and greed, much like the stockmarket has been recently, and go for the riskier, harder deal for a bigger return, instead of the safer, easier deal with a slightly lower return.

Think about how many of the second kind of deal could you do, with less effort, less stress and the faster returns?

The other thing they do is try to 'bend' a deal to work for them, rather than just going to look for another deal that does, effortlessly.

Gill Fielding, always used to say that she would always rather have the easier deal, leaving her time to get her nails done, rather than one big difficult deal where she would have to really work for her money.

And as someone who has 'bent deals to fit' on many occasions, I now have to agree 100%.

ACTION STEP

The first thing to do is create a yardstick for any deal you are considering. The ROI figure can be applied to anything and you can compare like for like, even if the deals are very different.

How much profit will a deal make in the first year, multiplied by 100, divided by the amount of money you are going to have to invest, to acquire that profit.

That, roughly speaking, is your return on investment expressed as a percentage. A house that costs £50,000 and will generate £2400k per annum of rental income profit, after expenses, roughly generates a 4.8 % return on investment. Not to be confused with rental yield, which is different again.

If you think that the property may grow in value by 10% that year, then add £5,000 to the £2400 rental profit, to find that your ROI is now 14.8%.

Compare that with a similar deal, where you can buy a business card printing machine franchise generating £25,000 per year profit and you have to put in £75,000 to acquire the business. 33.3 % ROI and you have to go round emptying the money. Worth it for those returns, you say?

But what if you had an 80% mortgage on the property, and the interest repayments were covered by the rent, still leaving you with the same rental profit per annum?

You have spent £10k to acquire that profit, you have a profit including capital appreciation of £7400k so your ROI is now 74%.

And no money collection. But whichever way, both returns are a bit better than the building society returns and both are 'Feed Me's'. Use your yardstick, don't change the goalposts and choose opportunities to fit your strategy or plan.

Catastrophe & Contingency Funds

Okay, we accept that we deserve to pay ourselves first. So what do we do with the money?

Your Catastrophe Fund

Out of our 80% salary, first, we must create a flow of about 10% to pay ourselves first and the first thing we are going to do with this money is create a Catastrophe Fund, in a different bank or savings account to our Freedom Fund. This is not money for unexpected, irregular and intermittent expenses, you know, the ones that we forget to budget for, and end up scrabbling to find the cash for, like a new lawnmower, auto repairs or ballet classes. No, this is for major catastrophes, such as divorcing, losing your job or falling ill, when perhaps your only other fallback would have been to turn to the personal loans or credit cards. Experts usually agree that this should be between 3–6 months living expenses or you may prefer to set a particular amount of money down here.

What would make you feel secure? £2000? £5000? £10,000 or even £20,000? This will become your second line of defence against incurring debt (see below for the first line). Use a different account with a 30 day withdrawal notice period and set up a standing order from your day to day account into this account. Remember, this is a limited time period payment – when your set figure is reached, you can divert this money elsewhere.

Tip: You could either start this with your entire 10% or do half and half perhaps, with half going towards your Contingency Fund.

Your Contingency Fund

Figure about £1000 for your contingency fund. This is an amount of liquid cash, money you can get your hands on in 24 hours for the minor emergencies in life. We are talking boilers blowing up, camshafts breaking (who knows what they are but I know they're expensive!) or perhaps the roof leaking and needing to be fixed fast, before the insurance will pay up. Remember, this is a finite payment, when the Fund is full, you will divert the monthly amount put into it, into something else. Your attitude towards this fund will either make or break your new Financially Intelligent lifestyle. This is not a pool of money to be used for anything you fancy (like a holiday or a new coat), but a cushion amount that will be used, then topped back up from the Odds & Sods Fund (see previous section)

ACTION STEP

How are you going to set this up?

I will talk more about bank accounts on Day 30 but you should know that there are different bank products on the market that allow you to have as many different accounts as you like, called whatever you like. Why not investigate a few banks both on, and offline, to see if they have this facility?

Your Odds & Sods Fund

Okay, brace yourself. This is the tricky one to get your head around.

Before credit, people had to plan ahead. Whether you had a lot or only a little, you never spent all of it because anticipation meant survival. Then the easy availability of credit meant running out of cash didn't mean running out of money, leading us to think that being able to spend money was the same as having money.

Anticipation meant thinking only of the good things that were going to happen, like marrying someone rich, winning the lottery, or more basically, a pay rise, the monthly wage cheque, the next holiday. It didn't mean the unexpected trip to the dentist, the new shoes, the car breaking down. So we stopped anticipating, stopped planning, got sloppy. We started to consider occasional expenses as optional expenses and it's only when one rises up screeching and bites our bottom, does it become an essential expense.

We are using up and wearing out our cars, our clothes, our homes a little bit every day. How much are you thinking about the brakes on your car that are going to brake for their very last time in about eight weeks from now?

When the unexpected expenses come at us seemingly out of nowhere, we collapse in financial shock and have to reach for the credit cards, but really, they are not that unexpected are they? We just didn't do anything about them. But it is crucial to plan for those things as well and this is where the Odds & Sods Fund comes in.

ACTION STEP

Step by Steps Instructions

Step 1. Determine your irregular, unexpected and intermittent expenses. List them, and then estimate what you spent on each, in the last 12 months. Divide each by 12 to get a monthly amount and total up that monthly amount.

Step 2. Open up a bank account called Odds & Sods Account (or any other name you like). Set up a standing order for the total monthly amount as worked out above.

Step 3. Set up a mini day–book for each category in your Odds & Sods account, and when the first standing order goes through, enter the credit amount as your opening balance on each sheet.

Step 4. If you have to write a cheque for any category, enter it as a debit in that category. You will find at the beginning that sometimes

---

you will have to write a cheque that is bigger than the credit balance for that category, but it will usually be covered by the amounts deposited for other categories and it will go back into credit as you deposit the next month's totals.

Step 5. When you get used to using this method, enter any unexpected windfalls to this account but add them to a new category, a dream account. Add in dream categories like a new computer or perhaps a holiday.

Step 6. Your goal is to have a full year's requirement for any category in each sub–account at any one time. The best thing of all about the Odds & Sods account is that, when you reach the amount you estimate you spend in a year on any category, you can divert the extra to one of your dream categories.

WEALTH WARNING!

Beware of thinking of your Odds & Sods account as a savings account – it is not, the money in there is meant to be spent (on the planned things!) and it is meant to ebb and flow.

Financially Intelligent Bank Accounts

One of the things I have struggled with for years is the question of having different bank accounts for different activities (which makes sense) yet trying to keep things simple because as sure as eggs is eggs (sic), any money is invariably in the wrong account at the wrong time. I know that all the other living–on–the–edge–entrepreneurs will know what I'm talking about!

I needed a blueprint on how to design a supportive environment using my bank accounts. One that would be almost automatic, one that would 'work'.

The first glimmer came when I read US coach Mike Neill's 'Freedom Fund' tip; I think it's perfect for employed people who want to leave their job and start a business. To read it in full, if you haven't yet, come along to the website and sign up for your free 30 day trial at *www.TheMoneyGym.com/blog*

It covers setting up your bank account as if you were already self-employed and it's brilliant.

Then, just after this I was reading Mary Hunt's book 'Debt Proof Living' (which is excellent by the way), and she goes into bank accounts in great detail. A light bulb moment. Wow! I realised that if you combined this stuff with Mike's Freedom Fund tip, it would be a great blueprint for how to set up your bank accounts to be a support system, a new 'environment' to help you evolve into your new financial lifestyle.

And you can do that while earning interest on your savings at the same rate as you are paying on your mortgage. Better than any savings rate around.

There are even new bank account products now, where you can have several different 'pots', called whatever you like, with another account or 'pot' for the mortgage. Some even let you have a credit card account to use alongside the others.

At the stroke of midnight, they take all your balances, put them up against each other, and you only pay interest on your mortgage / credit card negative balance, less whatever credit balances are in your 'pots'. How cool is that?

ACTION STEP

Okay, so you have all the information. You need to find a bank where you can have different pots, with different names, but every day, they tot up your credit and debit balances and your mortgage/credit cards then you only pay interest on the combined balance.

If you are struggling with this concept, find a Mentor, a Coach or an Independent Financial Advisor who can explain it to you – it's just too crucial and too expensive to ignore it.

THE MONEY GYM WORKOUT PLAN

These are the actions I will take in the next month, arising from Module 3: Cashflow

1. _____

2. _____

3. _____

4. _____

5. _____

6. _____

7. _____

8. _____

9. _____

10. _____

11. _____

12. _____

13. _____

14. _____

15. _____

16. _____

17. _____

18. _____

19. _____

20. _____

Signed: _____ Date: _____

CHAPTER 4

Debt Busting

Good Debt -v- Bad Debt

Anyone who has read 'Rich Dad, Poor Dad' knows that good debt is defined by Robert Kiyosaki as debt that someone else is paying for you (a mortgage on a rented buy–to–let property for example) and bad debt is debt that you are paying for yourself.

Mary Hunt, in her excellent book 'Debt Free Living' has a slightly different slant on it, which adds to the above definition, I think.

She says that good debt is debt that is secured on something of value thus decreasing the risk for both lender and borrower. Ideally secured on something that will increase in value, not decrease. So in the event that you were ever unable to repay the debt, you would have something to sell, something of more value than the debt.

For Mary, bad debt is consumer debt, where you incur debt to pay for a depreciating item, something that may not even last three years before becoming obsolete, and where there is risk for both borrower and lender because the debt is unsecured.

She sums it up brilliantly by saying

'Spending money you don't have yet, to pay for things you (often) don't have anymore, is anything but intelligent. Nevertheless, that is what millions of people in the country are doing every day, every month, year after year.'

As someone who is probably still paying for a hi–fi I bought in the 1970's, due to what is called revolving credit (where you take out more debt to pay off old debt, albeit it at better interest rates or even 0% interest) I have to put my hands up and say I'm no angel here. But I have learned, oh, how I have learned. I would now no more incur any further consumer debt than run down Worthing High Street wearing nothing but a bikini made from Egg Cards.

Half of my clients are struggling with some kind of debt and the other half are generally debt free but so scared of incurring any debt at all that they are unable to move forward. They never get the power of leverage/gearing (other people's money) working for them.

I had the surreal experience of hosting a teleclass on this subject to three people who gaily informed me at the start of the class that they didn't have any debt at all. I was a bit flummoxed at that point. As we explored the topic of incurring debt to leverage your wealth creation and making sure that other people pay any debt for you ('good debt' in other words) I felt a little like the snake tempting Adam and Eve!

At one point, I was tempted to pay off all my outstanding debt when we sold a house. Then I wondered if I might not be better to buy an asset with the money, which will generate an income for life, and use the income generated to pay off the debt first and then afterward, put money in my pocket. A much more attractive idea, especially if the asset in question is a house in Greece!

I consoled myself with the thought that most of my debt by then was 'good debt' and the saying that, 'if you have half a million pounds worth of debt, then you are halfway to being a millionaire!'

ACTION STEP

Are you brave enough to face your debt and stop the rot?

The first step is to determine not to incur any more consumer or 'bad' debt. If you can freeze this moment in time and say, 'no more!' then you will have taken a huge step in starting to bust your debt. You can only start to reduce it if you don't keep adding to it.

If you are feeling really brave, just make a rough list of all the debt that you think you have. Your task over the next 10 days is to gather information about each debt. How much is it? What is the interest rate? What is the minimum repayment? Call and ask them, if you just make the minimum repayment each month, how long will it take you to repay it?

Debt Proof Living

This is going to be Mary Hunt's chapter, at least at the beginning, because her excellent book 'Debt Proof Living' has such a wealth of good advice. She talks about the 'Principles for Debt Proof Living' and I have tried to distil the essence here, but I would recommend you read her book too.

1. You must never keep it all (we have talked about tithing already).

2. You must never spend it all (this is the pay yourself first concept).

3. There are only five things you can do with money. Give it, save it, invest it, lend it and spend it. Notice where 'spend it' comes in that list. Last.

4. Accept that someone or something else is the source of your talents, intelligence, abilities and creativity. Your unique responsibility is to be a good steward of all that you receive and to use it to the max. Who are *you* not to shine?

5. What you receive is what you deserve. A rather controversial statement really, but when you think about it, why would you deserve more if you can't learn to do the best with what you have?

6. Mary Hunt recommends that you always pay cash. I'm not sure I totally agree with her here, because it is too easy to lose track of your expenditure if you pay cash. I prefer to think of my clients as grownups and it's better to learn how to handle the various tools like credit cards, switch cards and bank accounts, than not.

7. No (stupid or bad) debt, no matter what. Nuff said.

8. Develop a strategy/plan. This is so important and so many people don't do it. You need to write out your short, medium and long term objectives and then look at each and decide what actions will best serve your objectives. Then go and do it.

9. More money is not the answer. The more you have, the more you will spend and if you have to earn it then the harder you will have to work.

10. Pay in full now or pay twice later. Or even three times. And how profoundly depressing to think that you may still be paying for something that you don't even have the pleasure of using anymore.

Living without debt is like a tax–free increase in income. Do you remember the younger Nicola staring at her salary slip and willing the net amount payable to grow?

Well, if you can liberate the amount you pay to your loans and credit cards every month, then it is like giving yourself a tax free pay rise.

Powerful stuff.

ACTION STEP

What are the next steps?

Okay, so now you know how many debts you have and how much you have left to pay off. You have resolved not to incur any more consumer debt. If you want to buy something, you will find out what it would cost to buy it on credit per month, and then put that amount away until you can afford to buy the item outright.

Make a note of the total amount you are paying to service your debts at the moment, every month. Resolve that this is the amount you are going to pay every month, off one debt or another, until you have no more consumer debt left.

The good news is that it will make you feel better, because you know that, if you don't incur any more consumer debt, then that amount will never go up and in fact one day it will go down, giving you that tax-free pay rise.

The Debt Busters: Who Are You?

In the same way that Michael E Gerber maintains in his book 'E–Myth Revisited' that there are three kinds of people when it comes to starting your own business, Mary Hunt maintains there are three kinds of people when it comes to attitude to debt and she describes them as follows.

The Revolvers: A typical example is Debt Ridden Dexter and he rides the escalator of life. The only problem is that he goes the wrong way, trying to climb UP the down escalator. This sounds like fun at first (watch kids at the mall or shopping centre!) but swiftly gets tiring and stressful. Initially he can keep up but every other debt added is like an extra shopping bag, rucksack, suitcase, briefcase and box to carry. It gets harder and harder and he eventually becomes unable to keep up the momentum of the escalator. Eventually he ends up at the bottom, battered and torn; he possibly gets himself sorted out, but always he starts to climb again.

The Daredevils: They live from pay cheque to pay cheque, paying off their debts every month but never having any reserve. Occasionally they revolve their debt for a month or two (summer and Christmas are typical) but they usually get themselves straight again. Unless something horrible happens.

The DPL's: These are the debt proof livers, people who design their financial lives carefully, only using cards and loans only when they fit in with their strategy or financial plan. They don't buy on credit, invest before they spend and have plenty of reserves. Everything they do with their money is 'on purpose' and they live exuberantly and with confidence because they have their future sorted.

My friend Adrian is a very sophisticated example of a DPL and he recently staggered me by explaining how he put his household expenses monthly in a high interest savings account, while running his day to day expenses on his 0% credit card (with airmiles), paying it off at the minimum amount due from the high interest account. At the end of the term, he either pays it off in full from the high interest account or moves it to another 0% card.

He showed me how it works on paper, and he is effectively putting the cost of his life on hold for nine months, giving him the use of his money to work for him, in the meantime. I have to tell you that Adrian is a bone fide genius (tested in the top 5% of the population) and is very, *very* disciplined and organised. Don't try this one at home kids, unless you are very confident that you can make it work!

What kind of a person are you?

ACTION STEP

So do we pay off the biggest debt first, or the one with the highest interest charges?

Financial intelligence would suggest that you should pay off the one with the highest interest rate first, but somehow, at the beginning, it seems too hard. If you are the kind of person who might get easily discouraged, then start with the smallest debt first. You pay the absolute minimum on all others, and put the balance of the monthly amount you decided to commit, towards the smallest debt. When that is paid off, move that amount to the next smallest and so on. You can see that this will be like a snowball, gathering momentum until it's racing downhill almost effortlessly, taking your remaining debts with it.

If you are a person with iron willpower and the only reason you have debts is because of circumstances beyond your control; those circumstances having now changed for the better, then start with the debt with the highest interest rate.

Draw your debt busting grids, one for each debt, with a square for each payment and have some fun colouring them in every month.

The Eighth Wonder of the World

Albert Einstein described compounding as the eighth wonder of the world and if you need any more reasons to get rid of your debt, this segment should convince you. We are going to go into compounding in much more detail in Module 5, but you need to know what it is (don't laugh, I didn't *really* know for years) and how it impacts debt.

Compounding is paying interest on an outstanding amount, and then paying interest on that interest, and then paying even more interest on the whole lot of interest, and so on.

Imagine you buy a computer on a credit card or using store finance. It cost £2000 (or $2000) and the terms are 17.8% for argument's sake with minimum repayments of 3% of the outstanding balance.

At that rate it will take you (wait for it) 13 years and 9 months to pay the total price tag of £3759 (or $3759).

Do you really want to pay over one and a half times the amount and still be paying for it in 13 years time? I don't want to be still paying for my hi–fi I bought when I was 17, but I bet I still am.

Enough already!

I bet at this stage you are saying one of the following:

'But I needed that computer for my work.'

'But the interest rates are not that high.'

'I would never be that daft.'

'So what are you supposed to do instead?'

Find a way. Otherwise, when you want to upgrade your computer in four years time, you will still have 10 years left to pay on the old one. Then you slip into the 'can I afford the monthly repayment' mentality. You lose sight of the whole amount of the debt and just focus on the monthly repayment. You don't have a plan, you just cope from month to month and never raise your head over the parapet to be able to see the bigger picture.

That's what debt does to you, puts blinkers on.

ACTION STEP

The best way to make this personal is to do two things. Look at your credit card statement and see what you paid off it last month. Add up how much of that payment was interest, card protection, charges, etc. and see how much actually came off your balance. Even 0% cards find ways to relieve you of some of your repayment.

Then take one of your credit cards or loans and call and ask them, 'If I only pay the minimum payment, how long will it take me to pay it off?'

Leveraging: Other People's Money

So, enough about bad debt for a moment and let's talk about good debt, how you can use other people's money to pay for your assets.

Imagine you have £60,000. You want to buy a one bedroom flat to let out and can't decide whether to get a mortgage or buy it outright. Why would you even consider getting a mortgage if you could buy outright?

If you have one flat worth £60,000, and if it appreciates at 8% per year (conservative estimate) how much would it be worth in 1 year? 10 years? What about any positive cashflow?

Let's assume that your plan is to build up a 'stable' of buy–to–let properties and your goal is to generate income now, rather than create a nest egg for the future.

(Now bear in mind this section was written when buy to let mortgages were freely available, and may become so again one day, but in the meantime, the principle is sound!)

If you have six flats worth £60,000, and they appreciate at 8% per year, would you be six times better off? How much would they all be worth in 1 year? 10 years? What about any positive cashflow?

Would it be six times as much? Do the sums.

If you have £60k spare cash and you use that money to buy a £60k flat which generates an 8% per annum appreciation in value (conservative appreciation figure) with a £100 per month positive cashflow. At the end of one year you will have a flat that has appreciated by £4800. You will have generated £1200 positive cashflow in one year. You will be a total of £6000 better off in the first year.

If however, you use your £60k to put down a 15% (£9000) deposit on several flats costing £60k, you could afford six flats, or £360,000 worth of property. If that appreciated by 8% per annum, at the end of one year your appreciation figure would be £28,800. Again, if you generated a positive cashflow of £100 per month, if you multiply that by 6 flats, you have made in the first year £7200 positive cashflow. Add to your appreciation of £28,800. Total gain in Year 1 of £36,000.

£6000 better off or £36,000 better off? Six times better off in fact. You choose.

What about Year 2?

If you keep your one flat and it appreciates by 8% and generates £1200 positive cashflow, you will have made another £6,384 in Year 2.

If you refinanced your six flats to release the equity, you could get 85% (£330,480) of the new value of £388,800. You pay off the original £306,000 total in mortgages, leaving you still owning the original six flats, with 15% equity still in, and you have £24,480 in your pocket to go shopping for more flats.

You buy another 3 flats at the same price you paid for the first six (you are good at finding bargains now!) but have to stump up a bit of cash to make up the third deposit) and you now own nine flats, six that have appreciated in value by £31,104 in total plus a positive cashflow of £7200 (rent plus yearly increase, less the slightly increased mortgage), and three that have appreciated by £14400 in total with a positive cashflow of £3600.

Total gain in Year 2 using leverage = £56,304.

£6384 better off or £56,304 better off? Again, you choose.

And you are a lot better off in terms of tax, because all the interest paid on all your mortgages is tax deductible against rental income, as it is a business expense. Whereas if you buy something outright, you get taxed on all the income, as the Inland Revenue doesn't take capital repayments into account as a business expense.

Disclaimer: Obviously this example hasn't taken into account legal and valuation fees and costs of finance etc. but is just for illustration of the power of leverage. You should always get advice about your own personal circumstances and do the sums carefully, taking into account all costs.

ACTION STEP

What's your strategy?

You need to decide if using good debt would help you achieve your financial goals faster. Perhaps you are perfectly happy with no debt at all, perhaps you have all the income you need. That's fine.

But perhaps you would like to leverage a smaller amount of money to reach your bigger income goals faster. Are you being held back by your fear of *any* kind of debt? The best way to overcome fear is with knowledge. How could you get more knowledge and learn how to invest with confidence, knowing that you know how to manage good debt effectively?

Paying It Off

Now we are back to our own accounts and looking at the consumer debt we have run up over the years. A couple of credit cards here, a personal loan there, oh! and a nasty little storecard there lurking about hanging it's 17.5% APR head in shame.

Just how do you go about paying it off?

There are four rules for Mary Hunt's Rapid Debt–Repayment Plan.

1. No more new debt.

2. Pay the same amount every month, off each debt, until that debt is cleared.

3. Line up your debts according to size, putting the one with the shortest pay–off time at the top and the one with the longest term at the bottom. (Or use the highest interest rate/pay off first method).

4. As one debt is paid, take that payment and re–direct it to the regular payment of the next debt in line.

There is an example in Mary's book of the Green family and it compares different scenarios. They stick to Rule 1 (no more new debt) in the first but not the other rules, and it takes them 396 months or 33 years to pay off all their debts. They pay back £26k in debt but pay £18k in interest. A total of £44k.

In scenario 2, they obey Rule 1 and Rule 2 (pay off set amount) but they don't reallocate the amounts freed up when debts are paid, they spend the extra money. They pay their debts off in 73 months or 6 years and 1 month, saving £10k in interest.

In scenario 3, they obey all four rules. They pay all debts off in just 52 months or just over 4 years, and save themselves just over £11k in interest.

There you go, easy isn't it? Mary Hunt even has a rapid debt repayment calculator on her website *www.DebtProofLiving.com* so get the figures you need and work out how many repayments it will take to be free.

Easy, no? So why not? Why is it so hard for some people to do it, even when they know what they should be doing? Because life gets in the way, life throws curve balls, life sneaks up with exocet missiles. This is why your rapid debt repayment plan has to run alongside your Catastrophe, Contingency and Odds & Sods Funds. And all of that has to run alongside living in Financial Integrity.

Debt is the symptom of the problem, not the source. There is always a deeper reason why you are in debt, or have trouble clearing debt. Perhaps you are medicating stress with shopping, perhaps your partner is not supporting you in your striving for financial integrity, perhaps you don't have a compelling enough vision of what life would be like if you didn't have to service those debts.

Stop and think for a moment. If debt is the symptom then what is the source? Only by identifying that source will you come to see the solution. It may not be pretty.

ACTION STEP

If debt is the symptom... what is the disease?

What is the source of your debt?

Is it poor financial control? Is it unexpected redundancy? Is it constant yearning for a better lifestyle?

Try and see the source of your debt problem clearly – don't beat yourself up because you are in this situation, but do try and think clearly and honestly about why you are where you are financially.

Once you see the cause, you may be able to take action immediately, or it may be too difficult to tackle alone, so enlist the help of a friend, family member, or a reputable debt counselling service (who shouldn't charge you for the privilege).

Your Credit Report

Many of my clients say to me, 'But I couldn't do that, my credit record is terrible'. I ask them 'how do you know?' and they always answer that they have been turned down for something in the recent past. Or they have a county court judgement against them that they either settled years ago or are still paying off.

The same day that I was turned down for a credit card with a £1000 limit was the day I got the offer letter from my bank regarding the £300,000 loan to buy my hotel.

You just don't know what the criteria are for each lender. No two are the same. They have certain things in common that they look for and I'll go into those in more detail later.

Did you know that most people are turned down for credit because they are not listed on the electoral register? You can check whether you are listed at your local town hall or the equivalent in your country.

Don't guess and live in fear. Find out what your credit record is saying about you right now. There are two main credit agencies that hold details on people, accessed by lenders and this goes for the USA as well as the UK.

There is Experian and Equifax and you can obtain a copy of your current credit record for as little as £2.00 – I get mine sent to me, automatically, quarterly.

They will send you a little booklet that explains your record, step by step, and if even I (with my attention span of a gnat!) can read one, then you certainly can!

It's not so scary if you *know* what they are saying about you, and you have remedies if they are holding incorrect information about you. Knowledge is power remember.

In the current climate lots of people with exemplary credit ratings are STILL being refused mortgages, so don't worry too much if this has happened to you.

It can't last, banks need to lend in order to make profits, so why not, in the meantime, investigate one of the other methods of buying property (as covered in the Property Chapter).

ACTION STEP

Knowledge is power...

Look on the internet for www.experian.co.uk or .com for the USA. You can actually have a continuous monitoring service and it will alert you by email or SMS if anything changes.

Then visit www.equifax.co.uk or .com for the USA, they have a quarterly update service. Both of these services cost just a few pounds/dollars a quarter.

Repairing Your Credit

So you may have a negative entry on your report. A default or a CCJ perhaps. There are two things to know about the effect that this will have on your financial future.

1. You may be able to have it removed. You can have it removed if it is incorrect and the law defines incorrect as that which you 'reasonably believe' is inaccurate or incomplete, information that can't be verified or information that is obsolete. Consider your entry, does it come under any of those headings? If so, get it removed. If you can't get it removed, you may be able to put a short explanation on your record, explaining the circumstances. Be careful with this one as it can be a double edged sword.

2. If you have one negative entry, you will still get credit if you have several positive entries and they are more up to date. Lenders are so desperate to lend (because, if they don't, they don't make money) that they will assume one old negative entry is out of date, a dispute, or otherwise not to be trusted; if, and only if, the rest of your credit report is exemplary. So if you can't get the old entry removed within the six years that it has to remain, even if cleared, then work on your exemplary current credit record.

How can you build up an exemplary record?

Borrow and pay back. Borrow and pay back.

It also helps to keep your mobile on a contract and pay it immediately the bill arrives. My old Nan was actually refused a Damart catalogue because she had always paid cash for things, never owing anything to anyone. So she had never built up a credit record!

The Money Gym

Pay back more than the minimum each time, but never pay it off completely, move the same money around the cards even, but beware of applying for too many cards at once. Any more than two a month the alarm bells start ringing. Try and keep within 60% of your limit.

The reason you need access to credit while you are building up your financial intelligence is not so that you can go shopping, but to have access to funds for the time when you see that great opportunity.

If you can have one card or loan account that you only use to invest with, then the income from that investment pays off the debt for you, that's good or clever debt rather than stupid debt.

Mary Hunt, Robert Kiyosaki and Russ Whitney all go into this idea in a lot more detail, and give you step by step instructions on how to manage it carefully.

My two clever friends recently went to Spain to buy two houses. One to live in, one to rent out, the second to pay the mortgages on both. They had carefully built up their credit limits so that they would be able to put a deposit down on their cards if they found a bargain. They did, but the estate agency wasn't able to process their deposit because they had limits on how much they could accept on cards. Alan's credit limit was stratospheric! They still got their houses, they just had to send a cheque for the balance when they got home. So the money stayed in their bank account earning interest for another two or three weeks.

Don't Despair!

Don't despair if you have a terrible credit record or even if you are facing bankruptcy.

It really isn't the end of the world, as I found out when my credit record was ruined after I couldn't sell my hotel The Acacia for a year after planning was refused to turn it back into two houses (which I had buyers for!)

You can get a basic bank account which has cash point cards and often come with a debit card facility, so you can still buy things in shops, book hotels etc. These accounts allow direct debits or standing orders so you can still pay your bills.

Nowadays you can get pay as you go credit cards where you can top them up with cash online, this enables you to travel and book into hotels.

If you have one of these cards, they have a small monthly fee, and if you enter into an agreement with the company for them to lend you the whole fee for a year, then pay it monthly (as you would be anyway) it counts as a credit agreement and it even starts to repair your credit rating.

Keeping your phone on a contract helps with that too, as does making sure you are listed on the electoral roll every time you move – go to the council and make sure you are listed, fast.

ACTION STEP

Build up your 'Bargain Access Fund'.

Check your credit record carefully and address any negative entries.

A few years ago, if you are disciplined enough, you could start moving your credit balances around so that one card was always being paid off in full. Then we used to see how long it took for them to start raising your credit limit.

In the pre-credit crunch days, most of the time they would do it without even telling you. The trick was not to spend it on consumer items, but regard it as funds for investment opportunities – bargains!

Top 10 Reasons To Get Out Of Debt

Now remember we are talking about bad (consumer/unsecured) debt here, not 'good' debt.

1. Simple survival. If you are carrying a load of debt, even the slightest shift in your circumstances can leave you vulnerable. Think of the man travelling up the escalator the wrong way, with a briefcase, a suitcase, a knapsack, several carrier bags, a bunch of flowers, a hat, bag, coat and newspaper. All it takes is for his shoelaces to become undone, or for him to trip or get tired and it's all over.

2. Debt is very stressful. It can cause immense worry, sleep problems, feeling like a rabbit caught in the headlights, lack of control, the need to overwork, inability to enjoy time off, alcoholism, overeating, depression, inability to communicate with others, feelings of shame, powerlessness. Need I go on?

3. To protect your future. We have already said that every debt repayment is eating into your future wealth. It's not just the lack of money now, it's what you could be investing that money in, that would generate an income, that you are sacrificing.

4. Teach your children. One of my biggest drivers is to teach my kids about money and particularly compounding – its effects for good or ill. Your kids are learning to be world class consumers and they may well be learning to be world class debtors as well. Instant gratification is everywhere and unless you teach them how to handle those desires, they have no hope. You want better than that for them, don't you?

82

5. To protect Your Marriage or Significant Relationship. Remember that old game, paper, scissors, stone? Where stone kills scissors and paper kills stone? Here's another one for you. Money kills love, or more particularly, debt kills love. If half of all new marriages fail and 80% of the marriage breakdowns report financial difficulties to be a major factor (and it follows that other relationships other than marriage would follow the same pattern), you owe it to yourself and your lover to sort your debt problems out, before it's too late. On a personal note, this was the major factor in the breakdown of my marriage of 15 years. We just couldn't get past the very different attitudes to money.

6. To experience the joy of creativity. You may not think of yourself as a creative person, but I can assure you that you are. We all are. However, all the time that you are hustling to pay your debts, your creativity will lay buried under the stress, the worry, the busy-ness of life.

7. Make room for opportunities. Have you ever noticed that wealthy people have all the luck? Why is that? Could it be that they notice the opportunities all around us all, because they have more time and space?

8. Enjoy more leisure time. Being in debt and having no reserve is very time consuming. I'll come clean here and admit that I spent hours at my computer balancing the books for the hotel and reconciling my bank account because the money was never in the right place at the right time. If there weren't so many payments going out and more of a reserve, then I would have had more time. I could have done my accounts once a month without the need to keep such a close eye on my cashflow. It all came right in the end though as I've learned to manage my personal money with an 18-month spreadsheet so I have plenty of reserve and know in advance what impact every penny I spend today will have in three, six, twelve months time.

9. To be able to help others. If you are up to your limits, then you have no way of helping others. You are less likely to give money away to help your favourite charity, you couldn't respond to a family emergency...

10. There is a difference between giving it away and burning it! Why do you want to give your hard earned money to a faceless, nameless shareholder of a big finance company? Why are they more deserving of your money than you? Need I go on?

ACTION STEP

Did any of the above reasons to get out of debt resonate with you? I speak from the heart as I lived with debt for many, many years.

Make a list of the Top 10 ways your life would be different if you didn't have any consumer/bad debt right now? Make it personal, in the present tense and positive.

Then pin your list where you will see it every day.

Then resolve to make it happen – as quickly as possible.

Debt Consolidation

Many people ask me if they should consolidate their debt by re–mortgaging or taking out another loan to pay off old loans/credit cards or those with higher interest rates.

There are many, many advertisements on television encouraging you to do this and the arguments are powerful. When you are under pressure to make payments and desperate for a fresh start, the logic seems overwhelming.

The question I always ask my clients first is 'have your circumstances changed from those in which you incurred the debt?'

Looking back at my own past, my mother dragged us up out of the poverty pit by doing this, after she left my father and walked away with nothing but two small children. She married again (a wonderful man who I think of as my real father now – hi, Dad!) and they both worked full time, bought houses that needed work, we all moved in, they worked like stink outside their day jobs, doing up the houses, selling at a profit and then buying another wreck to renovate.

They moved over the years from their first property, a rundown rented house when I was 8 years old, via Wales and Scotland, to a large house in the best part of town when I was 18 – a house that, ironically now, became half of what was my hotel, The Acacia. Hey! Law Of Attraction anyone? I still wonder what lessons I was meant to learn from going back there!

The only problem was, while they lived in and renovated these houses, they were always living beyond their means and incurring debts (well, I suspect it was my mother who was!) and eventually they always had to sell, to realise the equity to settle debts, 'buy cheap' again and renovate.

I think my Dad would have liked a quieter life, to consolidate their gains and less moving!

My mum was over–optimistic; thought very big, overstretched in terms of buying one property at a time (a bigger one) and didn't have the financially intelligent tools and controls to prevent them going over budget on her renovations. It's not a question of blame because she did brilliantly considering a standing start but interesting to look back on in terms of my behaviour.

Boom or bust was the cycle and it was always about 18 months long. So we moved schools, moved homes, every 18 months. I am the only person I know who lived in about 10 houses in the same town in less than 10 years. We spent two years in Wales and two in Scotland so it must have been ten houses in six years. I became very skilled at making friends.

What I didn't realise for many years is that my mother was a born entrepreneur personality type (aha!) and I was repeating the pattern.

So, what does this have to do with debt consolidation? While I have used the 'consolidation' techniques myself, many times, I am coming to recognise that it is not a healthy way to live, financially. Most of the time, you can pull it off, but it's very costly, emotionally and in terms of stress levels, and with regard to your health.

This personal story will, I hope, encourage you to understand that unless you address the underlying reasons why you incurred debt in the first place, it's probably not a good idea to 'consolidate'.

These reasons fall into several camps:

- You don't earn enough
- You spend too much
- You have no control over or information about your earning/spending patterns so haven't a clue which of the above is true
- You know that you shouldn't spend like you do, but have some deep need that you are filling, even though you know you are not behaving in a healthy way

Until you address your reasons for incurring debt, consolidation isn't the answer. You will consolidate your debts and buy some time, at the expense of your personal growth, financially speaking.

Do you want to grow and change, or do you want to delay the inevitable?

ACTION STEP

So why *are* you in debt?

If you don't earn enough, get a better paid job or a second job.

If you spend too much, think deeply about why. Is this a compulsive problem or just that you never realised before what your outgoings are? If you don't know, go back to Module 1 – Discovery and do the homework so that you can find out what's going on.

If you are filling a deep need by overspending or financially sabotaging yourself then get some therapy and discover why. Once you know why, then you can choose to change and move forward and that is where coaching comes in. Bad financial management arises from either ignorance or low self esteem, generally speaking. If you know what to do (and you will, by the end of this book) and you still are not doing it... well, you could do worse than finding out why.

Or you can consolidate yet again, and put off sorting it out until next time.

THE MONEY GYM WORKOUT PLAN

These are the actions I will take in the next month, arising from Module 4: Debt Busting

1. _____

2. _____

3. _____

4. _____

5. _____

6. _____

7. _____

8. _____

9. _____

10. _____

11. _____

12. _____

13. _____

14. _____

15. _____

16. _____

17. _____

18. _____

19. _____

20. _____

Signed: _____ Date: _____

CHAPTER 5

Compounding

For You (Or Against You)

For me, compounding is one of the most exciting modules and the best one for turning clients into head spinning/exploding 'Scanners' style creatures. I give them the info, wait for the silences and count quietly... one, two, three... BOOM! Messy but fun.

Compounding was described by Albert Einstein (no stranger to head expanding concepts) as the Eighth Wonder of the World.

It's such a big concept that it's quite a challenge to get the magnitude of it across but I'm going to do my best over the next few segments. I would love your feedback as to whether I succeed.

Right, deep breaths all round. Here we go...

Compounding is where you invest a sum of money, either in a cash vehicle or in an asset, and the gain (or return) you make in the first year is added to the original amount invested and, in the second year, the gain you make is calculated and paid not only on the original amount plus the new amount (if any), but also on the gain made in the first year.

Clear as mud, right? You may understand the concept with your head but do you get it in your bones? The other problem people have with this is that they always equate compounding with the 4% return you can get from a building society. Forget that for a second.

Let's try again. I went to a Russ Whitney Property Seminar where I met an investor who said that he would never invest any money of his in a deal, unless he made a return of 100% every year.

How Does That Look?

If I invest £1 in the first year and I'm getting a 100% return/gain per annum, then going into year two I have £2. If the gain in year 2 is another 100%, then going into year three I have £4. Beginning of year four, £8. Beginning of year ten, £512.

Pay Attention – This is Where it Gets Interesting...

Beginning of year fifteen, I will have £16,384. Beginning of year twenty, £524,288. Beginning of year twenty five, £16,777,216. Yes, that's sixteen million, seven hundred and seventy seven thousand, two hundred and sixteen pounds. In 25 years, starting with one pound.

Ready? Hold onto your heads! Scanner moment coming. Imagine if you put in another £1 in year two? And another £1 in year three? And yet another in year four?

Oh, I can hear the squeals of disbelief now!

But where do you get deals that give you a 100% return? Deals like that don't come along every day! Or... I couldn't do that, I don't know how! Or... but what if the property market drops or there's a war (the current favourite).

Okay, I'll grant you, deals like that don't come along every day. But that guy on the Whitney weekend is finding deals like that every three or four months or so. How many deals like that do you want in your lifetime? How many £1's do you need?

We have just come out of the debt module so you know that debt is a terrible thing precisely because of the compounding factor. We have now seen that the compounding factor can be a marvellous thing too.

The question is, do you want it working 'for you, or against you?'

ACTION STEP

£1 a year. Could it really make a difference?

Do you think that you could find a way to liberate £1 a year to get to work for you, compounding away? Do you think you could be bothered to go and learn about ways to generate a 10% return on your £1 per annum, or a 20% return, or even a 50% return.

Are you feeling motivated enough to go back to your receipts and your files and your cashflow yet? Get your Freedom Fighter beret back on and liberate a pound or two.

Saving - v - Investing

I touched on this in the Discovery module but at the risk of repeating myself I'm going to go into it in a bit more detail.

But first, here's another little compounding story.

If you take a napkin just a miniscule part of an inch thick (one over 32 for the technically minded among us) and folded it in half and then half again, then again, assuming one were strong enough and had fingers that clever, how many folds would it take to make it reach to the moon?

Thirty eight and a half folds. Yet the moon is 238,900 miles away.

How far would it get if you folded it 50 times?

To the moon and back – not once but one thousand, one hundred and sixty two times.

Not a lot of folds between thirty eight and a half folds and fifty, are there? But a heck of a lot of difference between going to the moon once or over a thousand times.

This example illustrates very clearly why compounding is particularly powerful and you need to know that compounding is particularly powerful in the later years. Do you remember the drawing from the Discovery module that changed my life? The compounding/return on investment line crept along the bottom for ages and then it rose dramatically in the second half of the graph to cross over the outgoings line.

This is why everyone says that you should start to pay into a pension as early as possible and keep your money in there. But they don't really show you why in a way that most folk could understand in a meaningful way.

But pensions are another story!

If you can grasp the power of compounding and then change the word 'savings' into the words 'investment fund' then you will find it a lot more interesting finding ways to widen that gap between what you spend and what you earn.

ACTION STEP

How much do you think that you could free up to put into your investment fund? Why not take the amount you are currently spending on the lottery, that second takeaway per week, that extra cappuccino, and do some sums with a simple compounding calculator that you can create on Excel.

Just work out what you could save in one year by liberating some cash per week, and then play with some different % returns. You may even become a spreadsheet bore like I am!

I remembered that, when I worked in London, I used to have two large cappuccinos per day; one getting off the train at Victoria, and one getting back on to go home. At £1.80 each, if I just cut out the second one (made my mouth taste horrible anyway) for one year, I could have saved £468. If I had invested in property at an average (conservative) return of 10% per year, I would have made £3148 in twenty years. Not very exciting. But if I had done that every year, I would have made £62,960.

Still not very exciting? Let's not lose sight of the fact that I am only cutting out one coffee a day, five days a week here!

What Are The Chances of That Happening?

Did you know that, in 2003, figures reported that the average person in the UK spent £13 a week on the National Lottery?

I don't know about the USA, or countries in Europe, but I would guess it would be a similar percentage. Obviously this is an average so there are people like me who spend £0 per week and people who spend £26 a week. I'm going to go into percentages a lot more as it's one of my bugbears (I think they are public enemy No 1 when it comes to wealth creation), but for the time being hold that thought about the Lottery.

What about Premium Bonds or the US equivalent? Millions of people invest in Premium Bonds and I think they have worked out that holders of the maximum amount of premium bonds, £20,000, average a return similar to the worst performing 'safe' investment vehicle – the building society or high interest deposit account at a bank.

Smoking, now that's a game of chance. How much does the average smoker spend on cigarettes?

I'm not passing a moral judgement here but if cigarettes are averaging £5.00 a pack and you smoke just 10 per day, you will spend £17.50 per week or £75.83 per month. Statistics prove that you will have a very high chance of dying early of a smoking related disease, but if you do nothing else to increase your wealth, you will have a 100% chance of not becoming a millionaire in your lifetime.

So you don't smoke, don't drink cappuccino, haven't bought a premium bond and don't think of yourself as a gambler. Your money, say £10,000 or $10,000 is safely stashed away in a One Year Notice, High Interest, Free Woolly Hat and Ugly, Out Of Date Mobile Phone, You Can't Bend It Deposit Account. Paying a guaranteed 5% a year. Except that inflation is running at 2% so you are only actually getting 3%. You are a 40% tax payer so you are only effectively receiving £180. Hmm, who's gambling on their future now?

ACTION STEP

Congratulations! You have won... a 100% chance of becoming a millionaire in your own lifetime.

What could you (relatively painlessly) give up now that you know what your chances are? Does it feel real yet? I hope so.

Why not make a list of things you can live without to give yourself a 100% chance of becoming a millionaire?

How To Ensure A Comfy Old Age

A while ago, Gill Fielding, told me a story of how she was sitting in the dentist with her 13 year old daughter. There were few good magazines so they got talking and her daughter asked Gill how much she would have to save per month, in order to become a millionaire.

Gill said 'work it out' so her daughter spent 10 minutes or so doing some sums. She worked out that if she saved £1984 per month from age 18 to age 60, then she would have a million. Then Gill showed her that, through the power of compounding, if she just invested her money and achieved an average return on her investment of 12% per year, she would only actually have to save/invest £81.22 per month over the same period to achieve the same end.

Everyone who has children in the UK gets a child allowance. It's about £17 per week or £73.66 per month for the first child. If you took just £50 per month of that money and invested it, from the day your child was born until they were 18 years old (then you stop – they can earn their own money, right?) and achieve a return of 12% per year, how much would you have accumulated for your child at age 18?

£35,584. Enough for a deposit on a house, to send them to college, or set them up in a business.

Okay, so your kid is busy travelling the world, working as a ski instructor, hanging out of trees protesting about something or other. You despair of them ever getting a proper job and you are worried about their middle age, let alone your retirement! You decide to leave the money in the investment vehicle to provide for them later. You don't add to it at all. How much would they have at age 50?

£1.3 million! Outrageous!

You can make your children into millionaires in their lifetime just by investing their child allowance! By now, your lanky waste of space who was so unpromising as a teenager, has found their passion and are happily earning a living. You decide to leave the money for another 10 years, till they are 60. By then they would be worth £4.1 million.

Quite rich enough to look after you in your old age. I would write it into the conditions if I were you!

ACTION STEP

Do you really need the child allowance every month? Do you have two children?

Why not consider investing the allowance for your two children in a vehicle returning at least 6%.

You will guarantee your children's retirement even if they want to save the trees for most of their adult life!

Averages - Public Enemy Number One

Before I launch into a diatribe against averages, first, another little story to illustrate the power of compounding (no groaning at the back there!)

Now I'm not sure how true this story is but it goes along the lines of the American Indians being diddled into selling the island of Manhattan for $24 worth of beads, cloth, doodads and gee–gaws. If they had taken their $24 in Treasury Bills or a similar vehicle that incorporated compounding, they would apparently have enough today to buy back the entire island of Manhattan, one of the most expensive pieces of real estate in the world.

Remember, the average person in the UK spends around £13 per week on the Lottery. Including me, who spends nothing, and someone half as daft as my dad, who would spend £26 per week (work that one out). An average is designed to give you a feel for what most people/things are doing, designed to smooth out the peaks and troughs of human behaviour.

The FTSE 100 is a collection of companies whose shares can be bought by individuals and institutions on the open market. If they have 1000 shares issued and today's price is £10, then the company is valued at £10,000. Their share price moves up and down, according to profits reported, market sentiment about the products they have, the market sector they are in and a variety of other factors including the economy.

If the FTSE 100 is an average of the Top 100 most valuable companies in the stockmarket, and more share prices go down than up one day, then the FTSE 100 goes down, as it reflects the average share price movement of those 100 companies.

Does this mean that all 100 company's share prices have gone down? No. It means that some have gone up (sometimes by a lot) and more have gone down. Which companies do you want to invest in?

But if the FTSE 100 falls, it's doom and gloom all round.

If property prices rise across the country by 10% does that mean that all property in every area has gone up by 10%? No, it means that there are areas that have not gone up at all and areas that have gone up by 20%. Where do you want to invest?

There was a great TV show a while ago that pitted expert investors against novice investors, giving them an amount of money to invest in the stockmarket, over a set period of time. On average, the novice teams did much better than the experts at picking great shares to invest in.

Does this mean that all of the experts were rubbish? No. Does it mean that all of the novice teams were great? No. It means that more of the novice teams did well, than the experts. Who are you giving your money to, to look after?

ACTION STEP

Bringing it back to compounding, in a very circuitous way, I would be aware of two things.

If you choose your investment vehicle based on average returns, you will more than likely get an average performance.

If you learn well, and choose the vehicle that performs better than average, over time, the compounding effect will have a dramatic impact on your wealth creation and leave your more cautious (average) neighbour standing.

This week, listen with more attention to the word 'average', notice how many times the phrase is used and see how many averages you can notice and think for a second that that means there are some things performing terribly and other things performing brilliantly.

Doubling Up

Did you know that, on average (there are those words again) the value of a house doubles every 7 –10 years?

This means that any property, very roughly speaking, will show a return on investment of over 14% per year.

So why do people struggle so hard to pay off their mortgage early, to save themselves 3%, 5% or 7% a year, when they could use that extra money (or even reinvest some of their equity) to secure a 14% plus return on investment per year?

It's all most mysterious.

ACTION STEP

I would encourage you now to go back to the Assets & Liabilities table (remember in the first module? – Discovery) and attempt to fill in the future column. You know that property increases by about 14% per year, so take it a year at a time, and predict what you would be worth at some point, if you did absolutely nothing different and incurred no further debt. Pick a time in the future, say 10 years, and work it out for yourself.

Is that enough? It may well be. That's brilliant. But if not, which of the lanes on the wealth highway do you want to use, to bring you up to your target?

Serving More People

I once read in a very famous book called 'Think & Grow Rich' by Napoleon Hill that if you can just find a way to serve many more people, you will create an almost effortless flow of abundance in your life (money) and are almost certain to become more wealthy.

Many people have heard of network marketing, and its oft-associated evil twin, pyramid selling. I would just like to state for the record here that network marketing is a perfectly legal, legitimate and established method of moving product (pyramid selling moves no product, just moving money from lots of people to one!) marries the concept of serving many people with the concept of building a distribution network of other people, all working for themselves but you being able to benefit from their efforts.

So you find three people, who find three people each, who find another three people, etc., with each new level expanding dramatically (draw it out on a piece of paper). The fundamental principles are sound and there are many ethical and successful network marketing based companies out there (Virgin Vie makeup, Avon, Amway, Nuways, et al).

The argument most people come up with, to prove that it doesn't work, is that by the time you get to level 6, there are not enough folk left in the world. True enough, but many of the people in the network don't do anything so that saturation point just wouldn't happen. And there are more people being born than dying... yada, yada, yada. Always people keen to prove why things don't work rather than spending the time finding something that does.

I digress.

Those words about serving more folk struck me as important then and have stuck with me for years. One of the reasons I liked them so much was because of the underlying concept that becoming wealthy was not at the expense of lots of other people, but as a by–product of *serving* lots of other people.

This concept fits into the compounding segment beautifully, because if you can grasp the concept that you can serve more people, and all of those people know more people, and if you can turn that network of people into customers and a marketing team, then your possible streams of income are virtually limitless.

ACTION STEP

When I was a music manager and my only music producer act decided he wanted to be a video producer (bit of a disaster!) I realised that it was a bit of a lottery whether I could find another great act, whether they would produce great music, whether I could get them a record deal, and support them emotionally along the way. The popular wisdom was that you should only have one act, in order to do that act justice but it just didn't work. I started to think... how can I serve more aspiring artists than just one?

What other challenges do aspiring artists face? One challenge is to find a manager. Then I realised that the managers – like me – were struggling to find artists. And they were both struggling to find resources like recording studios, tape duplication places, photographers and stylists, backing singers, band members. All of the things that they need to even get a sniff of a record deal.

So I created a website that enabled people to register and look around for free, took their details, enabled them to search for each other but charged them a small annual membership fee to be able to contact each other. You could say it was like *DatingDirect.com* for unsigned artists, if you like.

ArtistManager was born. And for a long time, it made me money while I slept – until I fell out with the software guys and we had to close the site down. At one point it was serving upwards of 8000 unsigned artists, managers looking for artists and resources looking to serve both (and 30 new registered users every day). We enjoyed a 50% conversion from unique visitor to registered user, a 5% conversion from registered user to subscriber. We sent out a free email newsletter every month to bring them back to the site and encourage them to search again.

What do you know about, that you could use to serve more people, while you sleep?

The Butterfly Effect

When I first read 'One Minute Millionaire' by Robert G Allen and Mark Victor Hanson, I was struck by the story of the Butterfly Effect! Edward Lorenz was a research meteorologist at MIT and he created a computer programme designed to model the weather, via a series of formulas. Amazing concept in itself, right?

One winter day in 1961 Lorenz wanted to shortcut a weather printout by starting midway through and to give the machine the initial conditions, he typed some numbers from an earlier printout. Unexpectedly, his new simulated pattern deviated dramatically from the previous printout.

No computer malfunction – it suddenly struck him that, to save time, he had rounded off the numbers, and instead of using six decimal places: .506127 he had used just three: .506. He assumed that the difference, one part in a thousand, would have no real impact. He was very wrong. This tiny change in input has quickly created an overwhelmingly different output. The formal name for this is 'sensitive dependence on initial conditions' but the more popular name is the Butterfly Effect.

Or, simply put, that the tiny changes brought about by a butterfly moving its wings in San Francisco can have the power to change the weather conditions in Shanghai.

I loved this!

The problem I most often encounter – and experienced it myself for a long time – is that often people feel they can do too little or that it is too late to make a major difference in their finances. They don't believe deep down in their bones, that little improvements in earning power, or little economies, or putting by £1 or $1 a day can build up to create real wealth.

They don't take into account the power of compounding, the power of leverage or gearing, the power of the Butterfly Effect. Mike Filsaime's legendary internet marketing product 'Butterfly Marketing' took this to a whole new level a few years ago.

Or, simply put, that the tiny changes brought about by changing your spending habits, little by little, the tiny changes brought about by putting away a £1 a day in that jar on your desk, can have the power, one day, to change the financial conditions in your lifetime.

Nice.

ACTION STEP

'One Minute Millionaire' is one of the Top 20 most revolutionary books on Wealth Creation. Written in two distinct ways, within the same book, it deals with wealth creation for both right and left brained people, who have two very different learning styles.

It's in my personal Top 10 Life Changing/Wealth Creation books of all time.

So why not order the book and then visit the website at *www.oneminutemillionaire.com*

The Millionaire Equation

Wouldn't it be great if creating wealth was a question of following a formula? That idea really appeals! Well, here is Mark Victor Hanson and Robert Allen's formula.

Formula: A Dream + A Team + A Theme = Millionaire (Income) Streams.

Simple isn't it?

They go on to say

1. Dream: Building the Millionaire Mindset – self confidence and burning desire

2. Team: Attracting mentors and masterminding partners to help make your dream a reality

3. Theme: Selecting and applying one or more of the basic millionaire models for making money fast.

Or using my analogy, choosing which lane of the Wealth Superhighway you want to focus on first, and getting your first vehicle off the slip road of life and onto the road to riches.

Moving on, I would like to focus for a minute on the Team part of the Millionaire Equation.

By surrounding yourself with people who think like you want to, behave as you would aspire to, and take action like you are ready to, you will greatly increase – or compound – your chances of learning faster and taking action smarter.

The private discussion forum that comes with membership of The Money Gym™ is a brilliant virtual resource team to be starting with –

you will receive the details on how to join the forum when you stay on after your 30 day trial!

And in any endeavour, if you can build a championship team things will happen so much quicker than you ever dreamed of. Somehow, the synergy that is created when a group of people get together ensures that the results are so much greater than the sum of the parts.

My virtual R&D team and the team of people around me in each of my business endeavours, plus my marvellous friends and family, support and inspire me to greater things every day.

Thank you guys!

ACTION STEP

You have weeded out the energy vampires and started to attract like minded people to you. How can you take that one step further and create a championship support team?

Think about a project that you have identified as a possible earner for you – active or passive – as you have been working through the programme to date. Imagine this project ten years on, when it is massively successful, by your standards.

How does it look? Who is involved? What are the key personnel and how are they rewarded.

Write it all down as if it were a project family tree (see 'E–Myth Revisited' by Michael E Gerber for a great example of how to do this). Think of three key skills or qualities that you need to make your project work – who do you know already that has those skills or qualities?

Get really clear about the kind of people you want to attract and then start to share your ideas with the people you meet. Let them know what you are looking for and what you are offering in return.

See what starts to happen then...

Phew! Made it!

There it is – Compounding, the 8th Wonder of the World. Have I succeeded in making it sexy?

We jumped about a bit on this one so I will summarise the key points in a moment but first I would like you to think about a couple of key things.

The first is that there are Five Levels of Investor according to Robert Kiyosaki's excellent book 'Rich Dad's Guide To Investing'

1. The Accredited Investor

2. The Qualified Investor

3. The Sophisticated Investor

4. The Inside Investor

5. The Ultimate Investor

He goes on to say that if you are not prepared to learn enough to become even an accredited investor then you are not planning to be rich, but planning to be poor. An example he gives is where he hears people saying 'Of course, I expect my income to go down when I retire'. So many people plan for a retirement where they will be poorer than when they are working.

How daft is that?

Robert then goes on to say that the things you need to become even a basic level investor are the Three E's. Financial <u>Education</u>, Investing <u>Experience</u> and <u>Excessive</u> Cash. Excessive meaning more money coming in than going out – or your income exceeding your expenses.

The second key thing is one that is being experienced regularly by members of my R&D team, many of whom are members of the financial services industry.

I find one of the most often heard expressions when talking about financial intelligence is 'I know'. Many financial people 'know' the principles of wealth creation because they are faced with clients every day who have actually put them into practice. Generally, so many people already 'know' at least part of what I'm sharing here but so many of them haven't, to date, done anything with what they 'know'.

Or as I always say, there's a difference between knowing something with your head and knowing it in your bones. Don't let what you 'know' in your head stop you starting to 'do' because only through 'doing' will your knowledge start to sink into your bones.

ACTION STEP

We have decided that we want the power of compounding working for us, rather than against us. We have looked again at the difference of saving versus investing and how powerful compounding can be, if we just forget Public Enemy Number 1 – average returns.

We have found out how to make sure that our children are able to provide for our comfy old age, from the time they are babies, knowingly or not! We know that playing the lottery gives a one in something million chance of becoming a millionaire in our lifetime while compounding can give us a 100% chance.

We have learned that house prices usually double every seven to ten years (yes, as I revise this book in early 2010 after what most people perceive to be a house price crash, even now, house prices have MORE than doubled in the last 10 years!) and that you can make your strategy to look for deals that return 100% per annum on your investment (and that, like the supermodels, you don't have to get out of bed for a return of less than 30%). With just one less cappuccino or dropping just £1 or $1 per day into your jar, you can create a Butterfly Effect while planning to be wealthy or planning to be poorer. It's your choice.

Finding ways to serve more people, almost effortlessly, will create unlimited income streams almost as a by–product and you can find a way to do that. With your championship support team, your projects will start to move faster than you could ever imagine, while you create excessive cash, financially educate yourself and gain investment experience.

You won't let what you 'know' hold you back and you will put to work the Millionaire Equation.

The only question now is, knowing that every day makes a huge difference, will you start today or yesterday?

THE MONEY GYM WORKOUT PLAN

These are the actions I will take in the next month, arising from Module 5: Compounding

1. _____

2. _____

3. _____

4. _____

5. _____

6. _____

7. _____

8. _____

9. _____

10. _____

11. _____

12. _____

13. _____

14. _____

15. _____

16. _____

17. _____

18. _____

19. _____

20. _____

Signed: _____ Date: _____

CHAPTER 6
Equities

An Introduction to Equity Investing

With stockmarkets faltering all over the globe, everyone thinks that this is the worst time to invest in equities. What people don't realise is that the indicators used on the news and in the papers, the FTSE 100, the Dow Jones Index, the Nikkei, are all averages of the movements of a number of shares. Hey! It's our old friend, public enemy No #1 again – averages.

In this module I am going to cover some of the basics of shares, or equities; how to invest safely with a 'belts & braces' approach; help you understand the difference between fundamental and technical investing and how to spot a 'golden cross'; and what to look for in a company. I will give you a couple of simple but proven strategies and give you some further reading and online resources.

So while the FTSE 100 or the Dow Jones Index may fall, you will be able to take advantage of one of the four lanes of the wealth highway, without running the risk of losing your shirt.

Just because the FTSE 100 (and I will use this term from now on to describe any index, or list of shares) may have fallen, it doesn't mean that the share price of all 100 companies have fallen. It may mean that more have fallen than risen but it still means that the share price of some companies has risen. And it may be that they have risen quite dramatically.

And even more interestingly, the share price of a company is no indicator of how well a company is doing. Imagine a company that builds houses – it's a thriving, family owned business. They have strong management, treat their employees well with low staff turnover, they build quality houses, is growing turnover and profits year on year, have lots of capital and buyers snap up their houses as fast as they can build them. It also pays a good dividend.

Nothing but good news, but this company's share price is falling.

There could be many reasons for this. The 'market' sentiment may be against the construction industry as a sector, perhaps because of all of the adverse newspaper articles predicting the property market bubble bursting. There may have been another property company go to the wall recently, making hundreds redundant. It may just be the wrong time in the cycle for the construction industry.

105

If you were holding shares in this company, would you sell them just because the FTSE 100 drops?

The other thing to remember is that there are actually two reasons to invest in the stockmarket. One is to benefit from the hoped for rise in a share price. But that benefit can only be realised by selling. The other reason is to gain access to the income – passive income – that is generated when a company pays a dividend to its shareholders.

Yes, you get paid to own shares. Quarterly, half yearly or annually, you get paid a dividend, decided by the board of directors, usually calculated as a percentage of profits.

The first time I came across this concept was in historical novels such as those written by the Bronte sisters or EM Forster's Mapp & Lucia series of books. Any self–respecting hero's fortune was expressed as an annual income, usually derived from investments held by his family for generations. These investments would have been in property or in the stockmarket.

I've always fancied being a historical heroine with my own fortune rather than having to marry some Regency dandy to get at his.

ACTION STEP

A Simple Investing Strategy – Step 1

Buy the Sunday Times or your local serious Sunday paper and look for the Top 200 companies list in the Business section. Make a note of the ten companies with the highest yield and save the list and the paper till later.

Zulu Principle

Jim Slater, in his book, 'The Zulu Principle', describes how his wife read a four–page article on Zulus in Readers Digest. If she had then borrowed all the books on Zulus from the local library and read them carefully, she would have known more about Zulus than most people in Surrey. If she had subsequently visited South Africa, lived for six months with a Zulu kraal and studied all the available literature on Zulus at a South African university, she would have become one of the leading authorities on Zulus in Great Britain and possibly the world.

The key point is that the history of Zulus and their habits and customs is a clearly defined and narrow area of knowledge upon which Jim's wife would have quickly become an acknowledged expert. Not a very profitable activity perhaps.

Jim Slater's point is that you should consider becoming an expert on a tightly focused area of investment. He chose small companies likely to become high growth shares but you may choose a particular sector of the market, or to become an expert in a particular investment strategy.

But where to start, when learning about the stockmarket and equity investing seems like an overwhelmingly huge subject?

My mentor Gill used to describe learning about equity investing as having a line of tea caddies on the mantelpiece. One might be labelled unit trusts, one might be ISA's, one might be labelled investing in shares, one labelled investing in companies directly. Gill said that you should take one tea caddy down at a time and look inside, studying the contents carefully. When you are happy that you know all there is to know about that particular tea caddy, put it back and let it get on with its magic while you take down the next tea caddy.

If you just spend a bit of time learning the basics, perhaps practising with a 'fantasy portfolio' before risking any of the money you have liberated from your bills and non–essential expenses, you will be amazed at how 'expert' you can become. They aired a TV programme in Britain not so long ago, where they pitted investment experts against teams of three ordinary people. They gave all of them a sum of money and let them loose on the stock market. Guess what? Most of the time the teams made up of ordinary people beat the so–called experts in terms of share price growth.

Which sector or type of investment are you going to become an expert in? How are you going to do it? Perhaps pay to go on a course, or invest in a book. Remember the old saying? If you think education's expensive, think about how expensive ignorance could be.

ACTION STEP

A Simple Strategy – Step 2

Choose the five companies from the ten selected yesterday with the lowest share price.

Keep this list safe until later.

Investment Clubs

Many people get their first experience of investing directly in the stockmarket via an Investment Club. My dad not only invests directly but belongs to a club that meets once a month in his local pub. They are a bunch of curmudgeons who enjoy each other's company and they have a very rude name for their club!

There are many famous clubs including the Beardsmore Ladies in the USA and the ProShare UK website has a number of case studies like the Fyg Leaf Investment Club (short for Fenland Yoga Girls Learn Everything About Finance) formed from a group of ladies who meet weekly for a yoga class. The club came about because the group discovered a collective interest in learning about investing in the Stock Market. So that all eight members learn something and play an active role, each member has been given a job to do. The monthly meetings are lively, social and informative and are held over a dinner that each member contributes to.

The club's portfolio has had a bumpy ride since the start. Putting this down to volatile markets, the ladies are taking a long–term view. Having burnt their fingers on tech stocks, they now only buy in markets they understand and often favour local or small companies.

In the USA there is the National Association of Investors (www.better-investing.org) an umbrella group of 37,000 clubs.

In the UK, ProShare (www.proshare.co.uk) is the independent organisation that promotes wider share ownership and financial education. ProShare has assisted in the formation of over 10,000 clubs and provides a wide range of services for them including a help line, seminars, a quarterly magazine, a club website and a programme of awards and competitions.

Why not check out the investment clubs in your area and make new friends while learning the basics of investing. Investing with a club will usually involve a monthly investment of £20, £50 or so and doesn't stop you investing individually too.

ACTION STEP

A Simple Strategy – Step 3

Allocate an imaginary amount of money – perhaps £10,000, and make a note which shares you 'bought' in your wealth creation file. Write down the price you bought them at and how many you purchased. Every week, buy the Sunday paper again and see how your shares are doing.

Work out what your dividend income per year would be, roughly, using the yield percentage figure (the yield is the dividend divided by the current share price, expressed as a percentage).

Passive income, every penny.

The Belt & Braces Approach

When I was expecting my second baby, we found out that my husband had been left a portfolio of shares by an elderly aunt. We didn't know the first thing about shares but I had been watching a great TV series about a little old lady called Bernice Cohen who had turned £20,000 into an ever–growing nest egg of over £150,000 in just six years. I went out and bought her book 'The Armchair Investor' and I highly recommend it to you.

Bernice believes in investing in smaller companies with potential for growth in the share price and she talks about the 'Belt & Braces' approach when it comes to picking shares. She looks at both the fundamentals – the company product or service, its turnover, profits, growth rates, debt etc, and the technical side of things – the share price movements, historical and current, seeking patterns which may give a clue as to which way the share price might go.

I like Bernice's methods because she teaches you to look for certain criteria which show how sound the company is, as an investment; and then shows you what to look for in the share price chart, giving an indication of when to buy that share. There is not much point in buying shares in even the most profitable company in the world, if its share price is on a downward trend.

You do want growth in your portfolio, as well as a dividend, after all. For example, if you have 1000 shares in a company whose share price doubles over time, then you can sell half, realise some of the profits and invest them in a new share.

Are you feeling inspired to take that tea caddy off the mantelpiece yet?

ACTION STEP
Simple Strategy – Step 4

Every quarter, or half year, or year, repeat steps 1–3 and sell any shares that no longer fit the criteria, and invest in the new companies that do fit.

This strategy is called 'Dogs of the Dow' or 'Beat The FTSE' and has historically been very successful returning 20% year on year over the last 20 years in the USA and in the UK. £10,000 invested in 1979 and the dividends re–invested (compounding, remember) would have grown to £130,000 by early 1992.

Some Ideas For Picking Shares

My personal strategy is to look for companies who have managed to grow their profits by at least 10%, year on year, for the last five years. It's hard to make a profit in business – let alone grow the profits year after year. I think it's more important than turnover growth and shows strong management. How many high tech or internet stocks were showing a profit?

I want to see a low debt gearing ratio, so that the company's assets cover debts by at least once, and I want an upbeat Chairman's statement in the Annual Report.

I need to be able to identify with their core product or service – I'm with the legendary US investor Warren Buffett on this one – I won't invest if I don't understand what they do. I love to see that the board members are buying shares and not selling.

Then I look at the share price chart. Is the share price in a rising trend or just coming out of a slump perhaps?

I look to see what the 20 day, 50 day and 100 day moving averages are doing (I'll cover moving averages in a later segment). And I'm really happy if I see a 'golden cross' forming. More of that later, too.

I also use Sharescope (www.sharescope.com) software to update prices daily and give me access to a company's history. It's about £10 a month subscription and about £70 to download and it's invaluable. There must be similar software packages for each country.

When To Buy

When you are looking at a share price chart, you will see a series of zig–zags which will be rising, falling or moving sideways. What happens with a share price is this; if there are more buyers than sellers at any given point in the day, the price rises. Similarly, if there are more sellers than buyers, the price falls. If the share price is not moving much, or if the top peaks of the zig–zags are staying roughly level, there are as many buyers as sellers.

If a share price moves to a new high point, a certain number of investors will sell some or all of their shares, causing a bit of a drop. If there are good solid reasons for the first price rise, the share will quickly recover and possibly go on to new highs.

One way of smoothing out the zig–zags and looking beyond the daily trading, is to use moving averages. A 20–day moving average takes the share prices over the last twenty days, adds them up and divides by twenty. The next day the same thing happens. It creates a much smoother line and you can begin to see what the trend is over the last twenty days. I also like to see the 50–day and 100–day moving average. If they are all moving steadily up, one above the other with the 20–day MA at the top, then all is right with the share price movement. For the time being!

But the best picture is when a rising twenty day MA moves up through a rising fifty day or one hundred day MA. This is called a 'Golden Cross' and some people think it means that a share prices' fortunes are about to take a jump. Software like Sharescope can be set to alert you if one of your shares makes a Golden Cross, or you can search for shares that have had a Golden Cross in the last week, month, or year.

I sometimes trawl for Golden Crosses and then go and look at the fundamentals, starting with the profits growth over the last five years. Or I look for sound fundamentals and then go looking for Golden Crosses in the share price's recent history.

There are other signs to look for in a share price chart and E*Trade for example allows you to create moving averages when you look at the online share price charts.

There are many courses you can attend to learn more about both fundamental investing and technical investing. I like to combine the two techniques, spin my Las Vegas pendulum to see what the Universe says and then go for it. It's a lot of fun.

ACTION STEP

Pick one of the shares in your fantasy portfolio (or your real one, if you have some shares) and examine the share price chart. Is the trend up or down? Are the peaks largely rising or falling? Use E*Trade to look at the Moving Averages and see if they are sitting nicely, one above the other.

Or is the 20–day sitting underneath the 50–day or 100–day? If so, is it rising towards a rising 50 or 100 day MA? Good news if it is...

Your Strategy

It's time to think about your strategy. Do you want more income than growth? Or are you not bothered about income and willing to take few risks to grow your money? Smaller companies equal higher risk, but big ole' boys can go bust too.

Use a stop–loss percentage and stick to it. This is where you say to yourself, if my share price drops by more than, say, 10% in a set period of time (three days, one week, one month, depending on how volatile that share price is normally) then you resolve to sell it. You do not want to be lumbered with a company whose share price is dropping like a stone. Your money could be working more effectively elsewhere.

Bernice Cohen says if you win six times out of ten you will be doing well, because some of those six will do so well, the whole portfolio will grow.

Why not set a sum of money aside to play with, see if you can grow it and then if you are successful, set aside a regular sum to top up your pot.

Another idea is to set aside a sum to play with, grow it, sell enough to pull out your original stake, then carry on growing the rest. Then, if it all goes pear–shaped, you have lost nothing.

WEALTH WARNING!

Never, ever, ever be tempted to use money you need for something else. This is not a sure fire way to make money and in the early days, I liken it to controlled gambling. You know about as much as the average bloke down the pub knows about horse racing. But you will get better as you go along and I don't want you to get burned. That would be a tragedy because it will put you off using one of the four main lanes of the Wealth Highway.

Start with Unit or Investment Trusts if you must, use ISA's or other wrappers to protect your gains, but start taking those caddies down, one by one, and learning about them.

If, after a year, your portfolio hasn't grown by more than the Dow Jones or the FTSE 100, then go and find a good stockbroker and turn it over to them to manage for you. But for heaven's sake, stop listening to the share tipster down the pub, and give up on the dartboard method.

ACTION STEP

Decide whether you are looking for growth or income. You already have a portfolio (fantasy or real) of the highest dividend payers, so play with some smaller companies, perhaps from another index like the FTSE 250 or the Nasdaq in the USA.

Create another fantasy portfolio and buy another bunch of shares that fit with the other part of your strategy. Set a stop loss percentage and timeframe. Track those shares for a while and see how well you do.

A Real Example

As I write, I thought it might be fun to look at a real example. While this information will go out of date, you can use the criteria I use to look at any share tip in any paper.

This week's papers (Mail on Sunday Financial) are reviewing Wilson Connolly, as their latest Annual Report shows growth in profits, a record order book and possibilities of a takeover. Takeovers always drive up the share price of the company being taken over (and drive down the share price of the company doing the taking over!)

When I look at Wilson Connolly (WSNC) on Sharescope, I see that (apart from a blip in year end 2001), the company has shown double digit % profit growth since 1996 and that the forecasts are good for the next two years. The profits grew by 55% in year–end 2002 against a fairly static turnover growth so it looks like they have been concentrating on making the business more profitable.

The PEG is well under 1, which both Bernice and Jim Slater like because it shows that a share is undervalued and has room for growth in the share price.

What is a PEG and why is it significant? Brace yourself, techie explanation coming...

The 'earnings' of a company are the net profits after tax, attributable to ordinary shareholders. If a company has earnings of 10p per share, and a Price/Earnings ratio of 10, you would expect the shares to be priced at £1. If the company has earnings of 10p per share, with a P/E ratio of 20, you would expect the shares should be £2 and so on.

A company growing its earnings at 15% per annum would probably command a Price/Earnings ratio of 15, at 20% per annum a P/E of 20 and so on. By dividing the earnings growth rate into the P/E ratio, a PEG (price earnings growth factor) is established and the aim is to find companies with good fundamentals, an interesting share price graph (upward trend) and a PEG under 1.

A PEG under 1 suggests that the share price is too low, compared with what you would expect, looking at the rate of growth in the earnings (earnings are the net profits after tax, attributable to ordinary shareholders, remember).

The low share price could be down to lots of reasons, but it is usually nothing to do with the company performance itself.

When I look at the graph for Wilson Connolly, I see that the share price has been in an upward trend since the beginning of 2003, and all of the moving averages are aligning themselves correctly to follow the share price upwards. No golden crosses though. The consensus opinion is 'strong hold' which is encouraging. I would have preferred a 'buy' opinion from the brokers but that's not necessarily a turn off.

The price has just topped the last most recent high of 166 which is another good sign. It may, in the next month or so drop back as far as 155 as it seems to follow nice regular rises and falls, so I could set an alarm to see if it comes near that. However, Wilson Connolly looks like a nice solid share for the next year (2004) and I would probably wait till the price rises tomorrow, while people pile in on the tip, and then drops back slightly while some people take profits. During this gap I would seek out the Chairman's statement, then buy some when on the dip. I would be happy to buy at about 160p.

While I'm in Sharescope, I'll check out my Ted Baker shares. Ted Baker is a smaller fashion company who make great shirts – my husband and I used to own about 10 at one time! They have been a bit of a disaster for me because I bought them when the market was much higher, although luckily not at the highest price of £5.33!

I still think the company is sound, not least because Chris Barrow, still favours the t–shirts and Steve Watson, my business partner bought a jumper of his recently! The first thing I notice is that the consensus is 'buy' so that's interesting. The PEG is still well under 1 and the profit growth is still in double digits (over 15%) last year after a wobbly one year of only 3% profit growth in year end 2001. Forecast profit growth is good for the next two years; in double digits again.

It's all looking good until you get to the graph... horrible. The share price is in a downward trend with the moving averages lined up above it and the whole picture is upside down. Share price lowest, with the 20–day above, 50–day above that and the 100–day above that. Totally the wrong way round which tells me the share price is not going up in the very near future. Must just be the stock market wobbles and the fact that the fashion retail sector is awful at the moment.

A woman stayed at my hotel once who works for Debenhams and she said it was so quiet. All the time they keep talking about recession and the property price bubble bursting people won't go and blow money on clothes. Ted Baker's market is the twenty–somethings who will be struggling to buy their first home in this market. So I'll set a couple of alarms, one to let me know if the price sinks any further and one to let me know if things improve.

The sink in the share price does seem to be slowing in rate though so I might buy some while they are cheap to mitigate the price of the ones I hold already (this is called averaging down)

(TED BAKER UPDATE: I checked Ted Baker shares again in January 2010 when revising this book and hey! What do you know? The shares are back up trading at 480p – 540p so at some point they would have shown strong 'buy' signs if you were able to read the share price chart - see below).

The last thing I do is to go 'data mining' for some golden crosses. Sharescope can do a hunt through all the shares listed to see if any moving averages have performed a golden cross recently.

William Hill is one that comes up. The rising 20–day moving average has just crossed the static 50–day, but is about to rise through a rising 100–day. This echoes the share price trend upwards. So let's look at the fundamental details... consensus is 'buy', PEG under 1 which is a surprise for a bigger company like that, and the profits forecast for December 2003 are 281% – blimey! That would give the share price a dramatic boost. Looking at the profits over the last few years, it's seen dramatic swings from 18% in one year to 800% in another year. And a negative profit growth forecast for 2004. It's a bit all over the place but looks like a buy–and–hold till after the results are announced in December.

Unilever looks quite interesting, with a price hike from just over £5 in December to just under £6 recently. Again the rising 20–day moving average is about to cross a rising 100–day, and looking at the profits, the last two reported years show double digit growth with 60% forecast for this year. But the previous year's profit growth figures were negative – horrible. If I was a bit more of a gambler I would buy and hold for the year end, but my strategy is to only buy where there is double digit growth for the last five years, and positive profit growth projected for the next two, so I'll pass on this.

There you go, it's not rocket science and I find it rather fun.

One hour on a Sunday updates me and tells me if I need to take action on any shares I hold.

ACTION STEP

Check Your Portfolio

Have a look at the Sunday paper for this week and see how your fantasy shares are doing. Are you making money or losing it?

A Caveat

It occurs to me that I haven't covered any of the other, more usual methods that you can use to invest in the stockmarket. Tut, tut.

One of the major lanes of the wealth superhighway is the stockmarket. If you have a pension, then you are exposed to this lane, of course. This is actually one of the best routes, *for employees*, as for every £1 you put into your pension, if you belong to a workplace pension plan then your employer is contributing too. The government is also contributing via the tax breaks. This means that you totally shouldn't ignore this vehicle on this particular lane of the wealth highway. It's a bit like a Volvo. Large, comfortable, useful and safe.

There are also unit trusts and investment trusts (where a fund manager chooses a basket of share according to the type of fund you specify – high risk, high growth; low risk, low growth but high yield etc). These are more difficult to classify as vehicles as they depend on the model, make, year, and previous owner history you go for.

These vehicles, however, work marginally better than doing the equivalent of nothing, such as putting your money in a bank or building society, where your return is eroded by inflation. Or worse than nothing, gambling with your money in premium bonds or some other 'respectable' gambling scheme with no guaranteed return. This is like buying your vehicle from a car auction.

Working marginally better are ISA's and the myriad other tax efficient savings schemes. As long as you realise that they are savings schemes and not investments in the true sense of the word then you will know the kind of returns to expect. Not 30%, not 100%, not infinity % that's for sure. These savings schemes are the Ford Escorts of the investment world – without spoilers.

For self–employed people, there are many tax efficient options such as SIPPS (where you pay yourself a pension from your company profits – before corporation tax is deducted – and then choose where the pension fund will invest – often in commercial property for example). Hmm, now we are talking about an uncommon top of the range car. It looks great, is probably fuel efficient, but not very well known.

The problem with all of these more traditional forms of savings and investments seems to be that, most people, once they have a pension, some premium bonds and perhaps a 'rainy day' savings scheme in place, wrapped in a tax efficient wrapper, think that this is the end of their savings and/or investment opportunities.

They then hand all responsibility for their future abundant lifestyle over to some anonymous fund manager who, quite frankly, couldn't give a monkey's about the client's personal wealth. No–one ever cares about your money as much as you do.

Those more sophisticated investors I regularly meet, use all of the above *and then* add to them, with personally controlled and individually researched personal investments that suit their temperament and desired outcomes.

I hope that I have begun to expand your mind a little and encouraged you to think about higher returns, with lower risk, than simply leaving your money in the hands of folk with another agenda, or their own best financial interests at heart. It's worth educating yourself (even a little) as to how the stockmarket works. Anywhere in the world.

ACTION STEP

Read 'Rich Dad's Guide To Investing' by Robert Kiyosaki.

Pulling It All Together

So we have started a fantasy portfolio or perhaps decided that we could allocate a limited amount of money – money that we can afford to lose – for investing in the stockmarket. The aim is to grow the worth of the portfolio by more than the FTSE 100 or the Dow Jones rises over a set period of time.

Our strategy is set, either buying blue–chip shares paying good dividends for income, where the share price is undervalued (giving potential for growth) *or* smaller companies, with a sound trading history and a low PEG, where the share price does not reflect the potential of the company. Perhaps we want to mix the two strategies with half of the money being allocated to blue chips and half to potential growth shares.

We have bought our shares, set a trailing 10% stop loss, which means that we will look at our shares weekly, and if they dip by more than 10% off their highest price at any time, we will sell them to lock in our profits. We will only do this if there is some particular reason if the shares have dropped, not if the market as a whole dips because of some world news.

If they appreciate in value by more than 50% we will look at selling half of them to pull our original money out, to invest in another share.

We will have a wish list of shares that we have studied and are ready to buy. We have set the target purchase price for each, and have either opened an account with someone like E*Trade or Charles Schwab, or an 'execution only' account with a stockbroker.

We will make our own decisions at all times and be responsible for them, not leaving the building of our fortune to someone who now only knows a little bit more than we do.

We will keep our eyes open for companies that we understand, perhaps where we use their products or services and we will read the financial section of our Sunday paper, at least once a month.

In short, we are educating ourselves to be more sophisticated investors and we are having fun at the same time.

ACTION STEP
Useful Links

www.bigcharts.com

www.etrade.com / *www.etrade.co.uk*

www.motleyfool.com / *www.motleyfool.co.uk*

www.sharescope.com Sharescope Software

www.proshare.org Proshare – Investment Clubs Regulator, UK

www.better–investing.org National Association of Investors, USA

THE MONEY GYM WORKOUT PLAN

These are the actions I will take in the next month, arising from Module 6: Equities

1. _____

2. _____

3. _____

4. _____

5. _____

6. _____

7. _____

8. _____

9. _____

10. _____

11. _____

12. _____

13. _____

14. _____

15. _____

16. _____

17. _____

18. _____

19. _____

20. _____

Signed: _____ Date: _____

CHAPTER 7

Property

Why Should We Invest In Property At All?

Before we plunge into the Property chapter (one that inspires passion in most of my Money Gym clients - especially the women) let's look at why we should even consider investing in property.

We start by telling them that wealth creation is simple. It's not easy, because of the limiting or negative beliefs they hold. But it is simple.

Nothing could be simpler than becoming a property millionaire. Buy one x one bedroom flat worth around 100,000 in your local currency, per year for five years, stop, then hold onto them for 10 years, and voila!

You WILL become a property millionaire, who can, in later life, live off their property portfolio, tax free, with the portfolio growing all the time, involving virtually no work for the investor.

The problem is that nobody every believes that and their brain starts coming up with all the reasons 'why not' or 'I couldn't do that because...'

So we explain that investing in property is the 'slumbering giant' of wealth creation. Get your property portfolio started in your early days with us, by whatever means possible, as it will look after you well in later life, while you get on with creating short term income, usually via business, the internet and sometimes the stockmarket, then concentrate on medium term income streams and asset building, while your slumbering giant sleeps on, ready to wake and look after you in your old age.

So we show them how, if they just buy an ordinary little 'market value' property today, a one bedroom flat at say £100,000, and put a tenant in it, to cover the mortgage payments, it will be worth £200,000 in 10 years time, £400,000 in 20 years time, £800,000 in 30 years time and £1.6million in 40 years time.

As I say, they rarely believe us.

So we tell them to go an find a middle aged or old person, who bought and still lives in a property purchased in the 1950's or 1960's and ask them how much that property is worth today. That usually proves our point.

(For example, when I was 18 years old, in 1980, my friend Kim and I bought a four bedroom house in Worthing, for £27,500. That same house today is selling for £287,500. So every 10 years, it has MORE than doubled in value)

Then we tell them to buy five of these ordinary little properties, and in 20 years time, they will have a portfolio worth £2 million. With mortgages totalling £425,000, leaving £1.57 million to refinance and live on, tax free.

They usually get quite excited at that point, and some even fall off their chairs.

Why is property such a great investment, the kind of secure investment that the banks like so much, they require us to use it to secure any other borrowing?

Think about it in terms of supply and demand.

We all have to live somewhere. The social trend is towards more and more single people households rather than families, and more and more renting, as work and lifestyles become more flexible, short term and international. The projections for how quickly this would happen have happened more quickly than anyone expected, in just half the time.

So the properties in most demand are the smaller units; one bedroom and two bedroom flats and smaller terraced houses. People don't have the time for DIY and are reluctant to commute for hours so they look for convenient locations, good conditions and nice neutral decor.

At the end of the day, when it comes down to it, there are only three 'traditional' ways for wealthy people and institutions to put their money to work - and the wealthy need their money to work because that is how they became wealthy and become even more wealthy! The rich can't bear the thought of their money sitting around not earning its keep!

So, it's into property, into equities, or investing in businesses.

And the money moves around all the time, it moves out of equities when they are falling, into property. It moves out of property when the market moves down, into equities. And into businesses all of the time, because of the great tax breaks.

However, many poorer or middle class investors hold off from a first purchase, when the market is high (fearing a drop) or when it's low (worried it will fall further). This strategy of waiting for some sign from the heavens, is the worst kind, as it KEEPS them poor and middle class.

When I originally wrote this book in 2003/2004 I wrote that only that day, I had seen an article that says one in four first time buyers are holding off, waiting for the market to fall further, trying to read the 'bottom' which any sophisticated investor knows better than to try to do.

And the same is true in this amazingly weird market in 2010 – everyone is trying to call the bottom of the market, while the more sophisticated property investors I know are just hoovering up as many cheap deals as they can get their hands on.

As I said before, they have just released figures that show that, even in this market, property prices in the South East have MORE than doubled in the last 10 years.

The thing that happens then, with the inexorable rise of property, is that people cannot afford to buy as the prices always outstrip the multiples of their salary, because the other thing they are NOT doing, is working out how to create extra income streams, which would expose them to many more mortgage products.

How many times, when talking about 'buy to let' have you heard someone say that the 'bandwagon has passed' or that you have 'missed the boat'. The 'bubble is about to burst'. I heard someone that I previously respected a lot say something similar just the other day, to a whole roomful of people. I was shocked.

Many people live in constant fear of a house price collapse - and the papers feed that fear, the headlines are full of it. Good news doesn't sell.

When you look behind the headlines however, you will often find that they are talking about a slowdown in the rate of house price rises, rather than an actual collapse in prices. Some areas have had a correction, sure, but you will find those areas had experienced higher than average rates of growth, in the few years previous to this correction.

People have been buying property to rent out for hundreds of years - do you think the Gerald Grosvenor, 6th Duke of Westminster, landlord of Mayfair and Belgravia and the wealthiest man in Britain, reads those newspaper headlines or listens to that kind of talk?

Does Donald Trump, who has made several fortunes in property?

Gerald Cavendish Grosvenor owns 300 prime acres in Mayfair and Belgravia. Brought up in Northern Ireland, it was not until his early adulthood that he realized he was heir to an incredible fortune.

When his uncle died, his father inherited Westminster.

Yep, that's right, the whole of Westminster, London.

Other than the London sites he also owns 150,000 acres in Scotland, Lancashire and Cheshire where he lives in Eaton Park estate, which is over 11,000 acres. And guess what?

He's buying, not selling. People who make money in property make money whatever the market is doing. Because they learn the things they need to know, to know what they are doing.

What do you do if you own property and the prices are static or correcting, off a recent high? Don't sell. Here are the numbers to prove it!

Since 1956 in the UK the compounded average annual increase in house prices is 8.5% (source: DataStream). In the 32 years that the Department of the Environment in the UK have kept statistics, property prices have risen in 28 years and fallen in just 4 years. This includes two of the worst 'property crashes' on record.

Rents have risen on average by 13% since 1962 (Office of National Statistics). The average annual return on commercial property in the last five years, to 2002, was 12.3% (source: Property Databank).

ACTION STEP

Go and find some older people, ask them what they bought their first houses for, and the addresses, then go and find out what those properties are worth now. Do the same with any property you have owned. Prove the 10 year theory for yourself.

The Money Gym's Top 10 Ways To Make Money From Property

1. Drive up the value of your existing home (extend, improve, go into the loft, build a home office in the garden). Refinance it at the new value, invest that money in more property.

2. Educate yourself about what makes a good property deal, take deals to investors, charge 1.5% of purchase price as finder's fee. Build up your own deposit or investment fund.

3. As above but offer the deal to an investor for a 50% share, with the investor paying the deposit for the other 50% share. Split profits when refinanced and rented out.

4. Buy good quality existing housing stock, as is, to let to a tenant.

5. Buy property 'below market value' from a motivated seller and rent out.

6. Buy property 'no money down' and rent out. We'll cover how this works in more detail later!

7. Buy a 'reversionary' property at 50% discount - we'll go into those in more detail later!

8. Buy shops, church properties, old youth club association properties or post offices - anything being sold off cheap by a large property owner and changing it to a 'higher and better' use.

9. In the UK there were 8,000 rectories and parsonages sold off since 1945 and now the churches are selling off redundant churches. Since 1969, 900 of the country's 16,000 churches have been sold off, often well under market value. St Saviour's church in Knightsbridge, London, was sold off at £1.2 million, converted into a house and then sold for £5 million.

10. Buy 'below market value', renovate, refinance to get your money out, rent out to a tenant and go again, using your investment pot over and over again.

11. My personal favourite: Buy an option to buy a property at today's price in 2-3 years, for £1 or $1, rent it out above market rent to a tenant/buyer, pocket the cashflow, AND make a profit on the back end. I'll go into this amazing technique later in the chapter in the 'no money down' section.

Determine Your Strategy

I don't know where I had been all my life, but when I found out that you can have an investment strategy or plan, with regards to property investing, I was thrilled.

This is such a brilliant example of how simple making money can be. Not easy, necessarily, but simple. It will require some effort from you. And it will require you to open your mind and let go of many assumptions and negative beliefs.

What outcome do you require? What do you need right now in terms of outcome? What will you need in five years time? What will you need in 20 years time?

If you want income, you invest in smaller units in certain areas, that appeal to the most number of people. A good average profit to aim for, per month, is £100 net. If you want £1000 per month income, you will need 10 units. If you want £2000 then you will need 20 units.

If you want capital growth, then you invest in bigger units, in a different area entirely. If you want a mixture of the two, find smaller units that you can force up the capital appreciation on, by buying under value and renovating, then renting it out.

I was talking to a client recently who wants to create a property portfolio that will generate enough income to set her free from her job. She only has Saturday mornings free to look at, buy and then manage her properties so we decided that she should look locally initially.

Unfortunately, she lives in a desirable area in the South East, which has seen one of the biggest price rises in recent years. Great for her house value, not so great for her potential investments.

She did some research online and realised very swiftly that the average cost of a one bedroom flat is £135,000 and the average rental per month is £350 per month. Not enough to cover the mortgage. Interestingly, there are places in the country where you can buy a flat for £70,000 and still get a £350 per month rent. Or where you can buy a small two bedroom house for £35,000 and still get £350 per month rent.

Where is she going to have to buy, in order to achieve her objectives? Not locally, that is for sure.

It's simple but not necessarily easy.

Her next task is to liberate some time to do the research on potential investment areas. One is Leeds, in the North of England, where she has a good friend, so not only would it be a pleasure to visit on a regular basis, but if she found something that looked like a bargain, but couldn't view immediately, her friend possibly could.

Despite what 'they' say, I believe in mixing business with pleasure. You are more likely to take care of business if it's fun.

My personal initial short term strategy was to invest for income, then gradually (within three years) invest the profits for capital appreciation (five to ten years), then pay off the mortgages (ten to fifteen years) and then start to invest in reversionary properties. When I near retirement age, I will pull out all of my equity and start to invest again in income generating properties.

Initially, I will have to get off my butt and visit other areas - this is not easy for me as I have a limited amount of time. Or I will have to find property sourcers that will find good investments for me. How will they know? Because I will tell them what my investment strategy is. I know that I will have to make some effort to find a good management company, and build that cost into my figures.

But if you had asked me about a property investing strategy three years ago, I would have looked at you very blankly. It's just a plan to achieve your goals.

Thanks to my growing financial awareness, I now know 'what' I need to do, to achieve my goals. It's just a question of 'when' and 'how' I will do it.

Simple, but not necessarily easy.

So What If The Bubble Bursts?

The one thing that scares everyone thinking of investing in property is the idea of the 'bubble bursting'. Some even think it has burst already (I wrote this section in 2008 and there was worse news to come in 2009 but STILL in early 2010, according to The Halifax, prices had more than doubled since 1998 although the man on the street does not believe it).

However, in the 31 years between 1969 and 1999, a period of time that takes into account possibly the worst house price slump that most people can remember, according to the Department of Environment, Transport & The Regions (BSM/SML) statistics, house prices across the UK actually fell in just two years, 1982 and 1992.

One of my earliest wealth creation mentors (Gill Fielding made her early money by working really hard and buying property to rent out) taught me a mnemonic called 'A RIDE' to determine the likelihood of a house price fall. These are five criteria that they used to check off the current climate, if you like, with regards to house prices. One of the criteria for 'A RIDE' is the 'D' which stands for 'Demand' where there is still a demand for housing stock which will continue to hold prices or even push them higher.

Gordon Brown (Prime Minister in 2008) announced that, in the South Of England, we need 10 towns the size of Milton Keynes, just to keep up with demand. We need 250,000 a year to be built, and this year they are only building 80,000, due to the credit crunch. The demand is still there and rising with a bottleneck building up.

The other is 'R' for 'Ratios' where the ratio of house prices to average earnings was about 4 in 2003/2004, compared to 5.5 at the peak in the 80s. The long term ratio is 3.5 so that ratio was a little higher than the long term average - not high enough to worry about compared with the 80s. The current ratio is falling again due to the credit crunch.

The other 'A RIDE' criteria indicate that property prices may be about to stabilise, but the economic indicators are that there isn't a big correction due.

The other thing my mentor used to say (that always made me laugh!) is... So you own property and the house prices go down for a while. What do you do? Don't sell!

Our Property Story

My sister Heather and I bought a flat in 1988, just as MIRAS tax relief was being phased out and that (along with other things) created a terrific property bubble that burst around 1990. A central London flat, 1 bedroom, just south of Brixton, we bought it for £56,500. The value plummeted within two years to £36,000 and then my sister went travelling around the world singing, then she got engaged.

I met my husband (who lived in Notting Hill and thought south of the river was out of town!) so suddenly we had a flat that was worth nothing, that no-one wanted to live in. Her work came and went, I started businesses that tried and failed - we were really struggling.

I said many times that we should give the keys back (that was the standard way out of negative equity in those days) but, to her credit, my sister insisted that we let it out and stuck it out.

Interest rates climbed to 16% and we had to subsidise it because the rent didn't cover it.

At the worst, we however, we only had to put in £50 per month each. We managed. I had babies, she looked after it, the freeholder failed to maintain, we got involved in a four year court battle to force the freeholder to repair.

Heather carried the mortgage for a year or two - not easy.

Then, as the court battle came to an end, we realised house prices had risen in the last two or three years, to the point the flat was now worth £105,000. We made money without even knowing what we were doing.

Property investment is all about setting a strategy that suits you, making sure that strategy is sound and that you won't be forced by circumstances to make decisions that are unsound.

Remember the 6th Duke of Westminster's family. They've ridden out some price dips but they have also benefited from many more price rises.

Debt Unto Death

Did you know that the word 'Mortgage' comes from the word 'Mortir' which means 'Debt Unto Death'?

When I ask people to fill in their Assets and Liabilities table, they always put the full value of their house in the assets column, and the outstanding mortgage in the liabilities column.

But if you read Robert Kiyosaki's 'Rich Dad, Poor Dad' then you swiftly realise that an asset is something that 'feeds you' or puts money in your pocket, and a liability 'eats you' or takes money out of your pocket.

Where does property investment fit into that? Well, your house you live in doesn't feed you, so it's a liability. Extending on from that, the mortgage on your own house is a bad debt, because no one else is paying that off for you. So it makes sense to clear that bad debt as quickly as possible.

If you overpay a standard domestic mortgage by just £50 per month, it can reduce the term of the mortgage by 17 years. There's compounding working for you again. Or against you if you don't pay it off early.

There are banking products now that calculate interest payable daily; they allow you to offset the credit balance in your savings and current accounts against the outstanding balance on your mortgage - every day. You only pay interest on the combined amount at the stroke of midnight.

Furthermore, if you arrange to pay your bills at the end of the month, the increased credit balance is working every day to reduce the interest on your mortgage.

So what about Buy-To-Let property investment and mortgages?

Any property investment outside your own house should cover its costs and feed you, and don't forget that the interest payments are tax deductible, while capital repayments are not, meaning you pay tax on any profit if you pay down the mortgage.

In the early years, the tenant should pay the mortgage and costs, while the property appreciates, using an interest only mortgage to improve cashflow, while putting money in your pocket (feeding you). The mortgage on buy-to-let properties should be interest only so that your cashflow is improved in the early days, so that you can leverage every inch of the extra cashflow across other properties. This creates a compounding effect as covered in the 'Compounding' chapter of this book.

Later on, if you would feel more comfortable, you could swap the mortgage to a repayment one, and the tenant should pay down the (still good) mortgage debt to create an ever appreciating asset with a smaller debt on it. Later still, when the mortgage is paid off, the entire cashflow is free to 'feed you' when you need income again, when you want to retire.

Well, this was the way we USED to teach it in The Money Gym!

We have a much more sophisticated model now, which involves you 'milking' your investment for ever, taking out big chunks of cash, tax free, which you use to live on AND pay the interest only payments.

Going back to the different mortgage products on the market take a look at the kind of mortgage you have now, even on your own house. Does it calculate your interest daily?

If you overpay, does it make a difference to the amount of interest you pay?

If you pay your bills at the end of the month rather than the beginning, does it make a difference to the amount of interest you pay? If not, why not?

Think about the idea of buying to let with interest only mortgages. Does it terrify the living daylights out of you?

It takes our clients a while to get their heads around the concept of never having to pay their interest only mortgage off, and how much more beneficial from an inheritance tax point of view it is to leave a highly mortgaged portfolio of investment properties to their kids!

So, do you really 'get' the concepts of 'good' debt versus 'bad' debt yet? If not, read Robert Kiyosaki's 'Rich Dad, Poor Dad' again or perhaps attend a few of our teleclasses. It takes a while but it's so powerful when you get it, really get it, deep in your bones, and you can take action without fear.

Buying Under Market Value

It's a good idea to create a 'model', a bit like a yardstick against which you can hold up any potential property deal, to see how it stacks up. This way you can compare a one bedroom flat with a two bedroom house, you can compare a multi-occupancy dwelling with a new build offplan.

The way you do this is to devise your own 'Return On Investment' model or ROI.

The one I use goes as follows:

I work out the 15% deposit required (don't worry, those heady days will come again!), the amount of finance needed and the likely rate of interest per year payable on an interest only mortgage on the remaining 85%. I usually use 5% as a starting rate of interest. As I like back of beer mat calculations, at this stage I don't factor in legal costs, stamp duty etc., but you could if you wanted to. The key thing here is to decide what you are going to include, and stick to that formula for every calculation.

I then look at the gross profit per year generated by rental income, (you could factor in void periods and management agency costs here too) multiply it by 100 and divide it by the amount of deposit I will have to put down, to acquire that income generating asset. This gives me the basic ROI percentage and I look for deals generating at least 20-30%.

I then consider the area and roughly estimate the percentage that the property might appreciate in value over the next year, add that to the yearly profit, and do the sum again.

Then I think about any possible ways to increase the return on investment percentage, by buying the property for a lower price or under value (reduces my deposit required), finding a cheaper mortgage (increases the profit), renovating the property (drives up the appreciation figure), negotiating 'seller finance' or, as it sometimes called, 'vendor cashback on completion' (reduces my deposit so increasing the ROI figure).

So it makes sense to look for bargains in the form of properties that are undervalued for one reason or another, for sale by solicitors following a death, by divorcing couples or people who have to move quickly for work. Or properties that are 'cosmetically distressed' where the carpets are swirly, the kitchen and bathroom ugly and outdated, and where (for a minimum expenditure) you can drive up the value dramatically.

Or maybe the property is up for sale by auction. Properties end up in auction sales for many reasons but usually because the vendor definitely wants to sell; it forces a quick sale and completion is usually just 28 days after the auction date. None of the endless hanging about in a chain, being held to ransom by the first time buyer at the bottom, who doesn't really care when he moves because he lives with his mum!

ACTION STEP

Get your local paper, and a big red felt pen. Draw rings around all of the 1 bedroom flats in your area, no exceptions, then go back and list them on a sheet of paper. You will find a range of prices from X to Y.

Now go and group them into areas, the different areas of your town. You will again see a range of prices – in each area – from X to Y.

In each area, a property will jump out at you as being 'too cheap'. There will be a reason for that. Call the agent and ask about the property, how long has it been on the market, what it is like, what are the buyer's circumstances.

You will find a reason why that property is 'below market value' or BMV as it's known. Perhaps that reason would not stop it renting, or could be easily fixed.

Congratulations, you may have just found your first property bargain, hidden in plain sight!

Buying Property 'No Money Down'

This is the part you have all been waiting for! Just how do you buy property 'no money down'?

The expression no money down does not refer to 'no money at all' down but actually 'no money of your own' down. There are several ways to do this.

The first is by negotiating a good price (more than 5% off) for the property you want to buy. This will happen if the property is cosmetically distressed, the vendor is motivated to sell quickly (or even better, the vendor is what is called 'distressed' and needing to sell urgently). When the new price is agreed, tell the vendor that you want him to give you the discount on completion. This is often described as 'cash back on completion' or a 'gifted deposit' although the latter term has mostly fallen out of favour.

This allows you to apply for a 90% or 95% mortgage at the 'Fair Market Value' or 'List Price'. There are high street building societies that are happy to do this, as the property is actually worth the higher value (or it wouldn't have been up for sale at that price in the first place), you have just been clever enough to negotiate a discount.

In the UK you are allowed to have up to two residential mortgages, before you have to move onto 'buy to let' mortgages.

Let's look at a real world example. My sister Sarah, who is a bit of a property whiz given half a chance, found a cosmetically distressed flat, for sale by an absent owner, listed at £159,950. She negotiated a discount of £9,950, applied for a 95% mortgage of £151,952 against the listed price of £159,950, and at the completion date, will get £1,952 back in her hand. Enough to pay the stamp duty. The other way to do this, is to borrow the deposit on a loan, credit card (0% obviously!) or your existing mortgage, making sure that the rental income will cover not only the mortgage on the new property, but also the repayments on the loan, credit card or your existing mortgage.

You should factor in a % void periods, overheads and management agent fees but even if you only break even by that stage, the tenant is buying you an appreciating asset, that will generate a profit, when the loan, credit card etc. is paid off.

You might find a flat for £80,000, put down £4000 deposit (plus say £1500 for the stamp duty, legal fees etc) on your 0% credit card, take out a 95% mortgage for £76,000 at say 3.95%, on which your payments are £250 a month, but where you can let the property for £550 a month rent. Even allowing a void allowance of 10% per annum, plus 10% towards other costs, your rental profit will still be £440.

You make your repayments of £250, leaving £190 per month to go towards paying off the deposit, costs etc. In this instance, because you did the sums before you bought, you knew that it was a bit tight, so you manage the property yourself in the early days, until the initial deposit is paid off.

And finally, if you are buying a cosmetically distressed property, which needs painting, new carpets, perhaps a new kitchen and bathroom, you can borrow the money to put a deposit down and do the work, then either sell, or refinance at the new value, pulling out your original money and paying back the original loan or credit card.

Say you found a house for £120,000 which needed £20,000 worth of work doing to it, but which will be worth £160,000 or even £170,000 when it's renovated.

You borrow the initial deposit of £6000 plus the £2200 for stamp duty and costs, plus the £20,000 to do the work. You renovate the property, refinance at 95% of the new value of £170,000 (prices have gone up as well in the meantime!) which is £161,500, then pay off the original mortgage of £114,000, plus the loan or credit card amount of £28,200, leaving you £19,300. You rent the property out for £800 per month, which more than covers the new mortgage of £531 per month.

And do you know the best bit? You don't pay tax on the £19,300 because it is not income, it's borrowed money. Which the tenant is paying for.

It's so beautiful most people think it must be illegal.

Make Money & Help Old People Too!

When many people get older, they have bought their own house but end up unable to afford to live, due to not having provided for their retirement for one reason or another. This problem will only get worse, as many people find that their pension is not enough to live on, due to poor stock market performance.

Anyone who has read Robert Kiyosaki's book 'Prophecy' will know how true that is!

The only way for these people to live is to sell their family home and move to a smaller place, but this is the time of their life that they feel least inclined to move. And why shouldn't they enjoy their home, that they worked so hard to pay for?

Much of the time, the property has appreciated in value beyond all recognition, but that is no help to them, because they think they can't re-mortgage - too old, no income thus not able to afford the repayments.

Many people turn to 'reversionary' companies to help them find a way out of their dilemma. These companies arrange for investors to buy the property at a deep discount to the current value. The discount is often as much as 40-50%! Sometimes you get a mortgage for the balance, sometimes the company provides the finance, and sometimes the current owners do.

The benefit to the older people is that they are entitled to live out the rest of their days in their own home, with a lump sum of cash to spend and/or live on in comfort, while the investor knows that the profit is locked in at purchase and that they will further benefit from the inevitable price rises over the remaining lifetime of the occupant.

The occupant's next of kin must sign the contract also, to say that they agree (as this impacts their inheritance), but often they are so grateful that their parents will be secure and happy, that they are fine about it.

This is an investment for the medium to long term, as you will not be able to pull your money out. You will be unlikely to want to refinance as the occupants live rent free. But for someone who is looking for a ten year plus investment, growing at an average of 11% per year, it's a great deal.

ACTION STEP

Go to the internet and type in 'reversionary property YOUR TOWN' and see if there are any for sale locally. If not, expand your search a bit to YOUR COUNTY. You will, along the way, find the local companies specialising in your area, and you can set up an alert on their website, should any properties come on the market.

Buy To Let

Here we are - the most popular part of this section by far. You know by now that I like to start the sexiest sections with a few nice statistics - just to calm you down!

While all of these statistics are from the UK, I would guess that the information is largely true of not only the USA but also most developed countries.

According to the Office of National Statistics in the UK, rents have risen on average by 13% since 1962.

Countrywide Estate Agents in the UK have over 80 branches across the UK and they say that the average tenant is under 35, relatively new to their job, earn an average of £18,000 per year pay an average of £524 per month rent (outside London). What is the point of the above? Well, when considering buy to let, would you rather buy a property that is going to appeal to the most number of people, or the least? Why make things hard for yourself? The other thing to do, is to sit down and make a list of the things that would attract you, if you were looking for a rental property. Imagine yourself at 35, single, with a new job (sounds very attractive to those of us with children under 8, I can tell you!)

Look for some outside space, garage or off street parking, nice clean common parts, rooms that get the sun, a safe feeling about the surrounding area, local shops for the basics. Avoid noise in the form of traffic, neighbours, an airport or local night clubs / super pubs. Avoid low lying areas (flooding), parking facilities through gardens or dark areas and particularly flats above chip shops or other fast food outlets!

In 1996 in the UK, 10 million households contained married couples and 6 million contained one person only. By 2016, this is predicted to be 6 million households with married couples and 10 million single person households. The number of houses in the private rental market has fallen from 12% of the total housing stock in 1981 to 10% in 2001. Where is the demand here?

Interestingly, when you compare rental returns, you will find that the smaller the unit, the higher the rental return. With houses containing furnished bedsits returning on average 19.3%, 1 bedroom units returning 12.5%, 2 bedroom units returning 11.5%, 2 bedroom houses 10%, three bedroom houses returning 8.1% and the 4 bedroom house returning just 6.3%.

The return is calculated by dividing the rental income into the purchase price and the inescapable conclusion is that the cheaper the property, the higher the percentage return. (Above figures are from 'Buy To Let' by Stuart Powers).

When you are looking at a potential property, calculate a 10-20% void amount, factor in 10% for 'other costs' such as insurances, repairs, ground rent, etc., and a further 10% for management costs - even if you are going to manage it yourself for a while. If the property still makes a profit, still puts money in your pocket, then buy it.

Check out potential tenants carefully. Take up references, including employer, previous landlord and bank. Check out your potential tenant with Tenant Verifier (owned by credit checking company Experian) who are available at *www.tenantverifier.com*.

Your responsibilities include making sure that any furniture complies with Fire Regulations, checking gas appliances every year, ensuring smoke alarms exist in buildings built since 1993, and ensuring repairs are up kept on heating and all amenity supplies.

Many people say that they couldn't afford to buy an investment property but forget that they only need to find the deposit (can be as little as 15%) the legal costs (often around £500), stamp duty or local taxes (in the UK stamp duty is 1% up to £250k) and a valuation fee (often paid by the lender).

If property in your area is inexpensive, don't assume the rents will be low as well, you may be surprised. Check out www.upmystreet.com to find average costs of property, then visit your local estate agent portal site to get an idea of average rental fees.

And finally, what about those who say that the bandwagon has passed, the bubble is about to burst, you have missed the boat? This is where your earlier work on beliefs, behaviours and attitudes will serve you in good stead. Ask yourself if the person offering the opinion is a property investor? Do they know what they are talking about or is it just an opinion? Ask them why they think that, and what they are basing their opinion on - what do they know?

Or are they parroting something they have read in the paper? Talking of the papers, look behind the headlines - read the articles properly and then make your mind up.

The Future

I used to think that I couldn't be bothered with property. It just wasn't exciting and I thought it would be hard work. Then one day it dawned on me, that the only real money I had ever made in my life to date, had come from selling property that I had accidentally made a profit on.

I used to think that it wasn't worth buying one x one bedroom flat to rent out, because what use was an extra £100 or £200 per month? A drop in the ocean. I never dreamed that you could have 10 of those flats, replacing my earned income and setting me free.

I had no idea that the compounding effect worked on property, that most property in the UK doubles its value every 7-10 years (doubled its value!)

Clueless!

And then I met some very wealthy property investors who use all the techniques outlined in this chapter and that opened my eyes. Real people, who look quite ordinary.

And recently I read Robert Kiyosaki's new book 'Prophecy' in which he talks about the 75 million 'baby boomers' reaching retirement age within the next decade, being forced to withdraw their pension money from the stockmarket to provide for their retirement via an annuity. He reminds us that there are not the same numbers of young people investing in the stockmarket via their pension funds, to replace the many billions that will be taken out of it.

Robert reminds us that the stockmarkets of the world are driven up when more people buy than are selling, and vice versa. It's the vice versa that we should be concerning ourselves with.

There are billions of dollars / pounds circling the globe every hour, looking for a place to get to work, growing the wealth of the world's wealthiest people and companies. When the stockmarket goes up, the property market goes down and vice versa. Again, it's the vice versa we should be concerned with.

Robert Kiyosaki does not say NOT to invest in the stockmarket or take out a pension. He just tells us not to rely on that retirement vehicle entirely. He recommends to invest in property as well, build a business as well, create intellectual property and attract customers via the internet, as well.

Remember Bernice Cohen's 'Belt & Braces' approach as outlined in the Stocks & Shares chapter of this book. Even as a risk-taker, I like the idea of many income streams and I have grown to love property as a tangible, touchable SOLID vehicle for my future financial well being. In fact, being backed by a solid property portfolio enables me to happily take some risks in building my business, creating my internet empire.

Why don't you think about it too?

2007 was the date that Robert Kiyosaki predicts will herald the beginning of the change in the investment climate. He thought that there would be a massive boom between 2003 when the first draft of my book The Money Gym was written, while people frantically pile more money into their pensions and perhaps the growth in property prices will languish a bit while this happens. Well, that didn't happen! But if it had languished, it would have been a great time to buy then!

Why not revisit your short term, medium term and long-term property investment strategy. Do you want income now, tapering off to capital appreciation later? Or the other way around? Or something between the two? Dig it out again, dust it off, get some education, read some books.

But for heaven's sake, do something!

I'm going to end this chapter with a funny true story that happened to me recently.

The Ladies

January is a month of many birthdays and I went to one of the birthday parties last night and what an amazing group of women there were! From the 70-something matriarch Liz, through my generation down to my sister Sarah in her mid-thirties, a good time was had by all.

About halfway through the evening, one of the girls, Eleanor, was asking me how the wealth coaching was going, and lamenting the fact that she felt really poor, and that her husband was approaching 60 but didn't see how he would be able to stop working.

I tried to resist, but in the end I caved in and asked her how much equity she had in her house (knowing she had lived in our area for years!) and what her mortgage was. She wasn't sure of the value but estimated it around £450,000 with a mortgage of around £10,000.

The Money Gym

When I told her that she was not only already financially free, but could be living a happy and wealthy life with her husband not having to work, she just didn't believe me. She knew she had a lot of money locked up in her house, but thought that you couldn't get a mortgage at their age (she's quite a bit younger than her husband, just over 50 I would guess).

Other women started to gather round me while I tried to change the subject, as I don't like to bang on about this stuff in a social environment, but they insisted so I asked permission of the hostess, my friend, who has heard all this a million times before, and she laughed and said, 'OK, go on then but keep it short!'

I went through the whole story, of how property doubles in value every 7-10 years, but how appreciation in our area will be quicker because they are about to build a big marina just by the town, and how we are benefiting from the doughnut effect of London, Brighton and Worthing, and the fact that we are an easy one hour or so commute to Victoria, London.

I told them how – in normal markets - you can mortgage up to 70% of value, without proof of income, and how you can put some of that money aside to pay for that mortgage for the next X number of years, earning interest on it all the while, and by this time, they were fascinated, but still not really believing me.

When up piped Liz, the matriarch, and said, 'Oh yes, she's quite right you know! We have always had an interest only mortgage, and we have all our cash in the bank, not in the house! We keep pulling it out, putting some aside to pay the new mortgage for a few years, and live on the rest.

'That's how we get to have so many holidays, how we keep getting the house done up (which puts the value up again) and I have just lent my other daughter a BIG pile of money to help her out. My BIGGEST problem is more about how not to have to pay too much tax on our interest we earn on the cash.'

Everyone was astounded, not least of all me!

'But Liz, why does Eric work then when he's getting on and could be taking it easy?' they all asked.

'To get him out from under my feet, of course, and because he would go stark staring mad if he was at home and bored stiff!'

And there you had it, someone who most people would say is a fairly ordinary woman, a woman who, in their 70s, her whole life knew instinctively how to do extra-ordinary things with money and more particularly with property.

And suddenly, I was much in demand for coffee.

THE MONEY GYM WORKOUT PLAN

These are the actions I will take in the next month, arising from Module 7: Property

1. _____

2. _____

3. _____

4. _____

5. _____

6. _____

7. _____

8. _____

9. _____

10. _____

11. _____

12. _____

13. _____

14. _____

15. _____

16. _____

17. _____

18. _____

19. _____

20. _____

Signed: _____ Date: _____

CHAPTER 8

Profit From Your Passion

How Can You Profit From Your Passion?

This chapter is all about the concept of profiting from your passion by developing a business online from something you love.

I have had to totally rewrite this chapter in January 2010 as internet marketing (and mentoring SMEs on how to take their business online) has become one of my greatest passions.

I'm privileged to be the only British woman to be asked to speak twice at The World Internet Summit and one of the co-founders of WIS, Brett McFall has become a friend and mentor of mine.

In fact it was difficult this time around to separate these two chapters – Internet & Business - at all, as when I originally wrote them, in 2003, making money online was really only in its infancy while the concept of successful business was being extensively explored in books like 'The E-Myth Revisited'.

So I've tried to focus in this chapter on how people without an existing business can make money online (see my '7 Quick Tips' on getting started later in the chapter) and how people with existing businesses can take those online and add to their profits without adding to their overheads.

To set the scene, here's a report I wrote especially for 'real world' businesses to get a feel for how important it is to create an online strategy.

You will notice that it's written in a very different style to this book, as this book is designed to teach, while the report was written as a marketing aid for my business, and the 'most wanted action' for the report, was for the reader to click on either the link to my website, or the links in the report.

Business Success 21st Century Style

If you are a solo professional, entrepreneur, freelancer or even an SME with several employees, the most important thing you need to succeed, in the crucial first few years of your business, is new business.

And lots of it.

Then what you need to keep going in your business – and to be able to build a business to love - is lots of new business coming from your ideal customer or client.

Let me ask you something...

Do you feel overwhelmed and scared when you think about marketing your business yourself?

Are you stressed out because you need more sales, but your budget prohibits a big, fancy marketing campaign?

Would you love to hire an expert but don't know where to go, who to trust or how to afford it?

Do you wonder how your competitors afford to do the advertising they do?

Perhaps you've heard that 50% of advertising doesn't work but most people don't know which half?

Have you heard that you only get a 1% response to direct mail at best?

Tell me this...

Would you love to find about an affordable, automated, comfortable, proven system to send your marketing stratospheric and make your sales and profits explode?

You would? Great! Then read on...

New business comes from effective marketing (lead generation), effective conversion of that marketing effort into potential customers (lead conversion) and then conversion of that potential customer into an actual customer (closing the sale).

But most new business owners went into business to DO that business, not to become marketeers or sales people.

They haven't got a clue about what to do, what works or how to do it effectively.

They are uncomfortable with the very notion of marketing or selling - and are terrified of doing the things they perceive they have to do, to be successful at it. Cold calling for one!

They also don't really want to talk money, negotiate or be seen as pushy or salesman-like. Or throw money away on advertising that doesn't work most of the time.

Well, I have some great news for you.

If this sounds like you, then you don't have to do it the old fashioned way. The terrifying way, the pushy way, the way that doesn't work most of the time.

Would you like to find out the most effective strategies, the most powerful tools, what your customers really want and will pay for, what really works?

Would you like to explode your bottom line profits for a tiny investment in time and money, and set into place an automated system to create new sales leads, to convert those sales leads into 'potential future customers' and then encourage those 'potential future customers' to become not only customers but raving fans?

Let me ask you something else...

We all love working for ourselves because of the freedom and flexibility self-employment offers.

Who doesn't? It's great, isn't it?

But sometimes there's just so much to fit into your day! You're running here, seeing people there, answering the phone here... and then it's late at night and you're wondering where the day went!

And there was just no time in that day to market your business was there?

Apart from the fact that it was the last thing you really WANTED to do.

Here's the secret to self-employment and SME success: Marketing doesn't have to be scary, hard work, expensive or un-enjoyable!

Once you discover what works, what you love to do, and how to reach the largest numbers of people with your marketing message effortlessly and automatically, you can do magical, natural marketing on an ongoing basis on an absolute shoestring!

And there are 1 billion potential future customers out there, on broadband right now (source: Sunday Times, March 2006) so what are you waiting for?

And if that isn't enough to get you excited about using the internet to reach your future business then let's see how you like the following amazing facts...

Here are some amazing – but true – internet statistics supplied by good friend, international business speaker, internet marketer and star copywriter Alan Forrest Smith (*www.OrangeBeetle.com*)

INTERNET BUSINESS FACT: There are 928 million internet users in the world as of June 2005, according to data published by Internet World Stats (interesting fact when you think how BUYING online is going through the roof! The market is hungry... you just have to feed it!)

INTERNET BUSINESS FACT: More than 75% of web buyers don't care whether an online store is run by a large or small company. Source: TNS, 2004 (so you don't have to be another Amazon to make cash!)

INTERNET BUSINESS FACT: $1.6 trillion was made via e-commerce in 2003; $7.1 trillion is expected in 2007. - Source: IDC, 2004 (no wonder so many web millionaires are being create faster than the whole of last century!)

INTERNET BUSINESS FACT: Nearly 100 million adults made purchases after doing online research last year, coming close to the number of adults who purchased through catalogs, direct mail ads and telemarketing calls combined

INTERNET BUSINESS FACT: Small businesses who use the Internet have grown **46% faster** than those that do not. (American City Business Journals)

INTERNET BUSINESS FACT: More than 724,000 people say that eBay is their primary or secondary source of income. Another 1.5 million individuals say they supplement their income by selling on eBay, according to the July 2005 survey. *Survey conducted for eBay by ACNielsen International Research. (and when you discover the truth about selling on eBay it's an outrageously easy way to create an instant business on the web)*

INTERNET BUSINESS FACT: According to Package Facts, rich consumers are more likely to shop online. Overall, 34% of respondents said they made an online purchase over the last year while 50 percent of mass affluent respondents and 57 percent of the highly affluent used e-commerce. (The web is a massive buyers market you can get a slice of when you know exactly how!)

Marketing Cornerstone #1:
Finding The Suspects (aka Lead Generation)

Why Build A List?

What your business needs to succeed is a mailing list. An ever-growing, personally owned, responsive, great big mailing list. A mailing list of thousands of people not just hundreds, is the goal. Not the word responsive.

This list is not only the place that your future business is going to come from, but it's an asset in its own right. People rent or buy leads for a one time use from anything from £1 a name to upwards of £100 a name (financial products).

A responsive, large mailing list adds to the intrinsic value of your business, along with your systems; making your business more appealing to potential investors, or your exit strategy more attractive to any potential purchaser.

(You do have an exit strategy, don't you?)

Ownership of your own list not only ensures that you never have to pay for leads, but you can create another source of income from renting your list out to complementary, non-competing businesses.

Most businesses start out with just one product or service and then develop further offerings down the line. By having a simple 'Product Funnel' which moves from Free to Low Cost to Medium Cost to High Cost, you can move your list gently through the process, enabling them to say yes, and yes, and yes again.

Almost best of all is that by creating your own list, you can market any future products or services to them, completely free of charge.

That's free marketing and advertising and it is almost unheard of in traditional businesses.

Building A Great List (Not Just A Great Big List)

The first thing you need to do is collect names and email addresses of your suspects (or 'potential future customers' as I prefer to call them) in return for something of value. This is called subscribing to your mailing list.

You probably gave me your name and email in return for one of my free reports from my website. I put a lot of work into my reports, to make them as valuable to you as possible. You have to deliver real value or people feel conned and unsubscribe.

This subscribing process needs to be effortless and easy, for you, as well as for your 'potential future customers'. They need to be able to subscribe easily, change their information easily (people do change emails regularly) and unsubscribe themselves easily (people do change jobs).

Trust me, you do not want to be doing this manually and it puts people off subscribing and annoys them intensely when they can't unsubscribe automatically.

The other thing to think about here is your Privacy Policy. You need one, it needs to be public and it needs to be carefully worded. Think about your end goal – are you going to be using you list for your company exclusively?

The next thing you need to do is to collect more contact information such as addresses and phone number, in return for something of even greater value.

Free teleseminars are great for that, or Free Preview Evenings, even low cost Open Days.

After someone subscribes, you need an automated follow up system and this can be done with a series of pre-written emails called autoresponders. They go out to the subscriber at pre-determined intervals and can be customised with the customer's name.

Our top tips for autoresponders are to send a message containing information of value every day for the first two weeks, then every three days, then every week.

Only market one thing to the subscriber in the first series of autoresponders, and this should be your Free Tele-Seminar or Preview Evening.

Keep things simple. When people 'buy' your free product, you can set it up so that they are unsubscribed from the first autoresponder series, and subscribed to the next one, marketing the low price item next.

You can also schedule automated broadcasts to go to some, or all of your mailing list. Ezines are sent this way, and special offers.

Traffic, Traffic, Traffic

However, none of this can be achieved without traffic to your website. There are many easy and affordable ways to drive traffic to your website without spending a fortune on the overpriced services offered.

Offline

Offline, you can do various inexpensive yet effective things to promote your website and drive traffic to it.

Use your Business Stationery – particularly your letterhead, invoices and business cards. Make sure your business card addresses the pain that your ideal client is feeling. Make sure it speaks to them not shouts about you. Put your photo on your card – that really helps people remember you.

Put something on the card to intrigue the reader and encourage people to go to the website – like 'Visit our website for a free White Paper PDF report on...' You don't even have to write the report yourself but can also use a ghost writer from www.Elance.com

Make sure your business stationery is current. You would be amazed at how many networking events I go to, where people give me their cards, and the first thing I do when I get home is try to look at their website to find out more about them, and it's not there! Or it's the wrong web address! Or there is just a holding page - or even worse an 'under construction' sign!

Networking

Networking is great for building advocates for your business. It's a bit nerve wracking if you think you are going to get a sale but if you go in to each event, thinking that your only goal is to add value, help other people and share resources, it becomes a lot easier and even fun!

Your ideal outcome from networking is to enable people to know what you do and who your ideal client is, and for them to have experienced some of your expertise. However, networking is very time intensive considering the numbers of people involved, so you need to remember that each of those people knows another thirty odd people, then it will feel more worthwhile.

Public Speaking

Speaking to crowds of your ideal clients is one of the best ways to drive traffic to your site. It's the USA's most popular phobia incidentally, but if you can overcome that fear, speaking in public is a great way to become a perceived expert, to get in front of a lot of people at once, and you can offer an incentive from the stage to encourage people to visit your site and subscribe to your list. One of my speaking mentors is Brett McFall, co-founder of World Internet Summit, a brilliant speaker and I'm proud to be the only British woman to be asked to speak TWICE at WIS UK, in 2006 and 2009.

Meta Tags

Meta tags are small bits of code that sit in your index page HTML source code, and tell the search engines what your site is called, what it's about, how often to come back and crawl your site, and what your relevant key words are.

To see some good and very effective meta tags, visit any of our sites such as *www.TheMoneyGym.com* or *www.NicolaCairncross.com* or my business partner Steve Watson's site *www.SteveWatsonOnline.com*

Just click on the grey background part of the site, and click 'view source'. You will see our meta tags there and you are most welcome to copy and paste them into your site, amending as appropriate. If you have a site yourself, right click on your index page to see if you have meta tags, a meta description or not, and if not, fire your web designer!

Try a search on Google for Nicola Cairncross and you will see how powerfully my sites have been indexed over the years.

Frequently updated and relevant content also drives your site higher in the search engines.

Blogs

We find that attaching a Blog (web log or web diary) to your site, and linking back from your blog to your site, creates a virtuous circle that the search engine spiders can move around. Every time you create a new 'post' on your blog, the blog software 'pings' the blog directories, alerting them (and the search engines) that there is new, relevant content on your site.

Low Cost Mailing Lists

Most town halls have a CD Rom or DVD based directory of local businesses which you can buy for a very small amount of money. You can then send a personal and direct email to each of those companies, with a short text-only message, telling the recipient what you can do for them (think benefit or outcome to the recipient rather than the dull old features of your product or service).

Encourage them to click through to your site by offering a free 'White Paper' report, to be able to attend a free teleseminar or preview evening or even to enter a competition. Team up with another local business to offer a prize of a meal out, a case of fine wine or a weekend away – it benefits both businesses and costs pennies.

Online Networking

Online social networks are becoming more and more popular.

I'm a BlackStar member of Ecademy and it's incredibly powerful. Ecademy is crawled by Google every hour or so (because it hosts a wealth of constantly updated content) and the first three lines of your profile will get indexed by Google very quickly.

You can link to your website from your profile, put ads for your products or services in the Market Place (and view and follow up all those who looked at your ad) and encourage people to visit your profile, give you testimonials and recommend you on to their network. You can blog on Ecademy too (I post all my blog postings to my own blog and my Ecademy blog), and contribute on the forums (called 'clubs') and the more links to your profile, the more people are likely to find you... and then visit your site.

You can get an idea of what's possible by visiting my profile on Ecademy here: *www.ecademy.com/user/nicolacairncross* and then also read a free report I created about the 'Top 10 Things You Need To Know About Ecademy'. Penny Power, one of the founders of Ecademy liked it so much she's directing all new Ecademists to it. See my 'Top 10 Things...' blog posting on Ecademy at *www.ecademy.com/module.php?mod=blog&uid=98913*

MySpace.com is gaining in popularity too, with many more adults using it now, although it's madly popular with kids and teenagers. Again, the point of having a profile on MySpace.com is that you can link to your websites, seed your profile with key words and it's crawled regularly by the search engines. And you can select your favourite music to play when someone visits your profile which is great fun. I'm in good company with my 'friends' on my profile too! See mine at *www.myspace.com/nicolacairncross*

I'm really into Facebook as it has some awesome viral possibilities and it's great for hooking up with people from the past (which can also be a bad thing!)

Facebook gives you the facility to create a media rich profile – see mine at: *www.facebook.com/NicolaCairncross*

You can also create a page for your business, book or product, that is visible outside Facebook and you can set it so that your blog feeds onto your page and updates it regularly.

Our Money Gym page can currently be found at: *www.facebook.com/moneygym*

Buying Traffic

I would recommend two books 'GoogleCash' by Chris Carpenter and 'The Definitive Guide To Google Adwords' by Perry Marshall. You can find links to both at *www.NicolaCairncross.com* on the Resources > Internet page.

And then you can attract traffic to your site within 15 minutes and you typically pay about 5 cents per click (always set your campaign in US $ rather than UK £ - it's much cheaper!)

So if you start from the average well-performing website statistics; your site needs in excess of 1000 visitors to convert 100 of those visitors to your mailing list and make 1 sale of a low priced product – perhaps an ebook at around £30.

If you are paying 5 cents a click, 1000 clicks will cost you $50 (around £27) so one sale will cover your advertising costs.

But the real sting in the tail – and the part that most website owners miss – is that you have acquired 100 warm leads to follow up, essentially for free!

Marketing Cornerstone #2:
Turning Suspects Into Prospects (aka Lead Conversion)

The real challenge with most websites is that they are just too confusing for the visitor.

Couple this with the fact that most sites shout 'me, me, me' when all the visitor wants to know is 'do these people *get* my problem, can they help me and what will it cost me?' you have a recipe for disaster.

Most websites are either created by web designers (ex graphic designers obsessed with design or worse, Flash!) or by techies (too hung up on the software). They are not created by internet marketers and they are NOT making money online.

So they don't know how to do that or how to help you do that.

Internet marketing is a lot like direct mail, except that it's much cheaper and instead of converting at an average of 1% it converts at an average of 1-10%. Like direct mail, it requires a knowledge of basic buyer psychology, copywriting skills, technical skill and the ability to track and test results.

Your web business should speak directly to your ideal client. Not any old visitor, or anyone, but to your ideal client. Your most profitable client, one who not only needs your solution to their problem, but who can afford to pay for it.

Your web business should offer a short list of options on each page – no more than three. 'Give us your name and email' or 'buy something' or 'click for more info'. This is called the 'most wanted response' online.

Your visitors should be very easily able to find what they are looking for – within five clicks ideally. They should be able to discover your range of products (no more than three initially) find out what they cost and get very clear instructions on how to buy or what to do next.

Your 'Terms & Conditions' should be accessible easily from your site and you must draw your customers attention to them prominently, with a notice to the effect that, by buying your product or hiring your services, they are agreeing to those terms.

Your web business must be 'sticky' thus encouraging the 90% of visitors who left without taking action, to return again, giving you another chance to capture their details.

Stickiness can be achieved by adding free resources, articles, relevant new content and making it interactive. Again, blogs are brilliant for allowing you to add all of the above easily and regularly – thus helping in your search engine positioning. Even large corporations are adding blogs to their sites – it gives the CEO a unique insight into and feedback from, the customer on the ground.

Creating a community around your web business is a very sticky thing to do.

Set up a free Google Group for your visitors and many will join that, rather than giving you their name and email, giving you another chance to interact with them and let them know that you have the solution to their problem.

Connect your ideal customers with a group of like-minded people and they will thank you and your good standing will be enhanced in their eyes.

Email support and discussion groups enable people to interact, swap resources, hints, tips and recommendations.

You are most welcome to join ours by joining The Money Gym and then visiting and participating in the discussion groups.

Talking of which, Membership sites are big business online.

Eventually you might be able to turn your community into a membership site – if your customers have common interests and concerns for example.

You offer a free entry level, then two further tiered membership levels. One at around £5 a month, and one at around £27 per month.

Membership software – including forums and support tickets for users, can be licensed and set up from as little as £50 a month.

If you can build your mailing list to 1,000 plus, then it's time to think about a membership site.

17,000 members giving you £5 a month = £1.2 million per year.

That's an extra stream of income not to be sniffed at.

We have set up a site to help people create membership sites, and you can watch a free webinar on the whole topic here

Find out more here: *www.MembershipClubMagic.com*

ACTION STEP

Think about what you could deliver, from your business, on a monthly basis, that would be worth £5 or $10 a month. A recipe? An interview with an expert? A 'how to' video either filmed via your webcam or camcorder or using Camtasia.

My sister has a blog that is not only chronicles her journey from overweight chocoholic to lean, gorgeous, vegan raw foodie, but she posts weekly diary / weigh in updates via video (which also get uploaded to her channel on YouTube) and she takes a recipe regularly and actually cooks it, filming the process and reporting her successes and failures. Check it out at *www.Rawrrr.com*

Marketing Cornerstone #3: Prospects Into Customers Into Raving Fans (Your Web Business That Works)

The first point of your web business is to collect the contact details of your potential future customers.

The second point of your web business is to set out, clearly and simply, your solution to the pain felt by your ideal potential future customer.

The third point of your web business is to allow your potential future customers to have a chance to get to 'know, like and trust' you.

People buy from people, and they especially like to buy from people they know, like and trust.

So many websites are impersonal, cold, impossible to navigate and even downright distant.

It's almost as if the owners are scared to be associated with their own products or services.

You need to be brave about letting some of your personality and character shine through your website.

The internet is popularly thought to distance people – stop them using the phone and face to face meetings, and many traditional business owners or sales people don't like it for that reason, use it that much or trust it particularly.

However, 1 billion people on broadband can't be wrong (Sunday Times, March 2006), and it is growing exponentially. The same article said that it was predicted that there would be 35 million Chinese people on broadband within 5 years.

We now know there are more Chinese people on broadband than there are people alive in the whole USA!

How do you differentiate your business from all the others?

You differentiate it by being uniquely you, by showing your 'you-ness' in your business and allowing that to show through via your web business and blog.

Many people feel that by showing their personality they are somehow being less professional.

But consider this, many huge corporations now run blogs.

Google allow Google staff to contribute on their blog. Bob Parsons, founder of GoDaddy.com, the biggest domain registration and hosting company in the world, runs a personal blog in which he shares business challenges, successes and musing. You can find it at www.BobParsons.com

Blogs allow your customers to get access to you and your company in a very friendly, informal way. It enables them to comment on your company (you can moderate comments) and reply to those comments.

Your website should have examples of what's called 'social proof', real live case studies and ideally testimonials of real live people who have benefited from your product or service.

Make them specific stories and not only include outcomes but how those people felt about the outcomes. You can see some examples of great testimonials on our site The Money Gym.

It's best if the folks that supply testimonials are willing to be contacted – it's a bit of a challenge with the Money Gym as members often don't want people to know about their money and how much more of it they have! It's a bit easier with my internet mentoring clients as we can include links to the clients' sites.

Always include full names if possible, website addresses (it's also a nice way to drive traffic to your clients' websites too) and contact details if the customer is willing – phone is best rather than email as it minimises the spam problem.

You can include testimonials and case studies in your ezine, on your blog, on your site, in your Ecademy profile, in your press releases... maximise everything you do.

How frequently should you contact your potential future customers?

A lot more often than you will feel comfortable with at first, that's for sure. The key is to be sure you are delivering value rather than selling to them.

I created a 101 day Financial Intelligence e-programme which I sold from my site initially. It was what turned out to be a life-changing programme, distilling the wisdom of many, many wealth creation books, woven in with my own experiences on my wealth creation journey and scattered with little exercises to do along the way.

I was looking for a way to set up an autoresponder series for new visitors to the site, without doing any more work myself, and suddenly realised that I should just give away the Financial Intelligence 101 series. 101 emails, one every three days... wow! That would remind potential future customers about the Money Gym for nearly a whole year!

Popular internet marketing wisdom says that, in the early days, a series of autoresponders should go out contacting new subscribers every day for the first 14 days, then reduce the frequency to every three or four days, then every week, then at least once a month.

Then you can add in broadcasts, at least fortnightly and ideally weekly, with an ezine full of value, or at the very least a snippet of an article of interest to your ideal future customer, featured on your blog, linking back to your blog.

You could also be adding content to your blog at least weekly. You don't have to write it yourself, you can use free online resources such as *www.EzineArticles.com* or even link to articles in the online versions of the daily newspapers. Another great resource is *www.IdeaMarketers.com*

As long as you link back to the source site and credit the author, there is not usually a problem. The more links incoming from other sites a website has, the more 'important' a site is deemed to be by the search engines, so you are actually doing the other site a favour!

You can see that, if you can create original content, or pay a ghost writer from www.Elance.com to do it for you, and your content is picked up and used by other sites, this will also improve your site's search engine ranking.

Which format should your broadcast be sent out as?

We have recently conducted a very interesting survey of our 10,000 subscribers. The results flew in the face of internet marketing wisdom.

Bear in mind that there are over 10,000 subscribers, divided up into mailing lists covering wealth creation, internet marketing, restaurant owners and work at home mums.

The ezine has been going since 1999, it's been very personal, it's been through several re-brands and even stopped completely for six months.

However, whenever I go to events, several people always come up and introduce themselves and tell me how much they love the ezine.

I regularly make thousands of pounds in commissions via the ezine, by gently recommending events, products and services that I already use or intend to go to myself. To date, I have never rented or sold my list to anyone else and always mail promotions with a personal introduction.

Survey of Our Readers

Do you read our ezine? 51% - yes 49% - no.

Do you like the new format? 67% say yes, 32% say no (good news for my new editor).

Do you prefer text only, HTML (magazine style with pics and links) or text with link to HTML online? 69% prefer it to come in as HTML (looking like a magazine with pics and links) 12% prefer text only 18% prefer text only with links.

How Do You Feel About Ads In Ezines? No, Hate Loads Of Ads - 41% Like To Know What's On Offer - 15% Don't Mind Them - 43%.

Marketing Funnels work very well. In the same way that you need a product funnel, to move folks from 'free to fee' products, in order to take these new leads you have generated and turn them into customers, you need a marketing funnel.

The whole purpose of a marketing funnel is move your mailing list subscriber gently from suspect to customer, in a series of natural steps, where the person at the other end is in control of the process.

The components of the marketing funnel are often similar, even for very different businesses.

Here is a suggested marketing funnel:

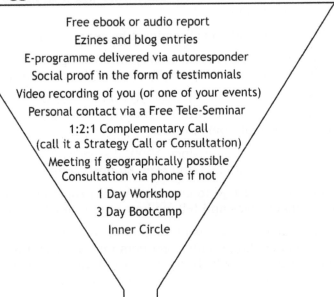

Free ebook or audio report
Ezines and blog entries
E-programme delivered via autoresponder
Social proof in the form of testimonials
Video recording of you (or one of your events)
Personal contact via a Free Tele-Seminar
1:2:1 Complementary Call
(call it a Strategy Call or Consultation)
Meeting if geographically possible
Consultation via phone if not
1 Day Workshop
3 Day Bootcamp
Inner Circle

People are very scared of committing themselves to a meeting or a purchase straight away, especially a higher priced item so you need to make it a gentle effortless process with the customer choosing when to move forward to the next stage.

When organising a meeting, if absolutely forced, I prefer to meet halfway if possible rather than going to the customer's office or home. This puts your meeting on an equal footing and seems less 'sales' orientated. If you don't value yourself and your product or service then you are setting things up so that the customer might not either.

The marketing funnel can be spread out over your chosen time frame, so it can be as short as a month, or as long as a year.

For example, people are joining our marketing funnel all the time, but if they join on the 6th of the month, they have to wait till the first week of the month until the next teleseminar and we only do our one-day workshops quarterly.

Conclusion

Unfortunately all of this means that, if you are starting from scratch and educating a market about a new product or service, then attracting actual paying customers can be more of a slow burn.

This can be frustrating for some, especially if revenue is needed immediately.

On the other hand, if you have an existing product or service, for which there is already a demand from an educated market, you can generate more revenue online very quickly using this system but you need to make sure that all of the parts are in place, and that as much of the process as possible is automated.

Then there needs to be a person at your company who is a bit techie, or a bit design orientated, and who loves to learn new skills - in which case they can learn to do all this for you. I warn you though, it's a bit of an uphill learning curve and it's not fast.

Or there needs to be an investment, and someone at your company who is willing to liaise with a company who can put all this together for you. And there are not many companies who can do it all, but there is one that I know of and they are not a million miles away!

Well, I wouldn't be doing a great job of our own marketing if I didn't tell you that we have the solution to your problem! Because of course we do.

But first of all, I hope that you will agree that I have shared some great information, and more importantly demonstrated that this stuff works.

In this chapter and the next, all about business, you will do some exercises to identify possible income streams and how to create an opportunity from resources, skills and knowledge you already possess. The concept of a dreamteam is not new to you by now but we will cover the concepts of effortless attraction when working on something you are passionate about.

We will begin to explore the highs and lows of being an entrepreneur and the double edged sword of the endless ideas flow, before reminding you of the massive wealth creation opportunities and tax benefits offered by creating a second business from something that you love.

ACTION STEP

How Can You Add To YOUR Bottom Line?

I hope the above report has inspired you to think about how you can use the internet to add to your existing business or business marketing?

Really it's all a matter of putting yourself in the shoes of your 'potential future customer'.

Take a piece of paper and draw a circle with your business inside the middle circle.

Draw 12 more circles with lines connecting them to the middle circle and brainstorm 3 ways you could add value to your existing customers and how you could reach them at no extra cost to yourself.

Fill another 3 circles with 3 ways you could add value to your 'potential future customers' and how you could reach them at no cost to your business.

Fill 3 more circles with ideas for creating new, preferably digital products, like MP3 audio downloads, PDF documents or webinars, that you could charge a little bit for, but use as a marketing / low cost product to draw 'potential future customers' further down the marketing/product funnel towards your main products or services.

Then fill the next 3 circles with people you like, respect and recommend, who may have mailing lists of people who may be interested in your product or service, but who are not competing with you directly. These are your future potential joint venture partners

Approach them with the thought of what's in it for them not you and you will get a good hearing, I promise.

But What If You Don't Have A Real World Business? 7 Steps To Take...

Quick Tip #1: Danger! You Can Earn Money Today!

The first thing I would do is put myself in danger of making some money from Day One!

I would go and find a product – perhaps the one I bought that got me interested in internet marketing in the first place, perhaps the product promoted by the speaker I saw that inspired me and find out if they have an affiliate programme,

I would join it, and then go to www.TinyURL.com or www.Bit.ly and shorten my affiliate link.

I would then add an email signature automatically to each email I send, from now on, and add a P.S to all my emails, with a link endorsing and promoting that product.

If I don't know what to promote, I would perhaps choose something promoted by someone I like and respect in the internet marketing world, and use that.

(You can find a list of the things I like and use and get a free report to give away and become an affiliate of The Money Gym at *www.themoneygym.com/blog/affiliates*)

Or I would go to Clickbank.com and select one of the most popular products from the Marketplace there to promote.

Then I would check every week, to see how many clicks I've generated from my email signature, and how many sales!

I would record that in a spreadsheet, even if the number of both is ZERO, because as we all know... 'what you focus on increases.'

Quick Tip #2: Get Active On Social Networking Sites

The next thing I would do is open my Facebook profile, and link it to my Twitter account (so that my Tweets appear on my Facebook profile) and update it regularly.

You do have a Twitter account don't you? If not, you need one urgently!

Twitter is like mini-blogging and is highly key-word searchable by the Search Engines - Google is even showing a rotating display of relevant Tweets on its front page when you do a key word search - try it!

Then I would start a Facebook page around the topic I am going to start my internet business around - think of your Facebook page as your first business website. It's visible outside Facebook and highly search engine friendly.

Choose a name for your Facebook page that has a key word or two, and says what it does on the tin.

So if you tweet regularly, and link your twitter account to your Facebook page, and you link your Facebook profile to your page, and then you Tweet on topic, you can see how you can start to generate some traffic to your new page, and hopefully some 'fans'.

This is the start of your mailing list and we all know that you can only start to make money online if you have a mailing list of people who know, like and trust you.

You can also occasionally recommend some of the products and services you endorse, using your Tiny URL or Bit.ly link.

Quick Tip #3: Buy Domain Name, Hosting & One-Click Install A Wordpress Blog

Due to lack of space, I can't even begin to go into why Wordpress is the way to go when creating your first website (a blog is actually just an interactive website and it can look just like an old style website too) but just take it from me, it is.

I'm sure if you Google it you will find endless arguments for and against, but I use Wordpress now and I love it.

I'll never forget when online audio & video guru Mike Stewart told me at World Internet Summit 2008, I think it was (I've never missed one!), that he had swapped to using a self-hosted Wordpress blog on his domain name. 'Why?' I asked. 'Because Armand told me to!' Mike replied.

Armand Morin (Google him!) is one of the most successful internet marketers of all time, and founder of the BIG Seminar, one of the best annual seminars in the internet marketing space. He is a genius and is surrounded by geniuses and if Armand is doing something one way, you had better know there is a damn fine reason for it.

So I hauled my 1000+ post blog off Typepad, where I was very happy but not getting any search engine benefit except for one link to my main site, and with one click on my server's Control Panel, installed Wordpress. A few theme experiments later and we are happy as anything with total control over our blog, which builds up search engine clout for us with every new post and comment.

If your hosting service does not offer a one-click install (often called Fantastico) then you can download the latest version of Wordpress completely free, from Wordpress.org, along with all the essential plugins and a massive choice of themes.

I maintain a list of the Top 20 Wordpress plugins I use (and the other 11 I wouldn't be without) here on my internet marketing blog and keep it up to date fairly often... *http://bit.ly/Top20WPPlugins*

I would recommend installing your blog in a subdirectory of your domain called 'blog'. This makes it easy for blog directories to find it (although you should also use a plugin to ping them regularly) and also gives you a bit of freedom about what you put as an index page in your root directory. You could split test squeeze pages (see below) or sales pages. You could host a welcome video... loads of choices but only if your blog is not in the root directory.

One of the features of Wordpress, behind the scenes in the Dashboard, is Widgets. There are various kinds of widgets but one of them (the Text widget) allows you to drop bits of code into your blog sidebar and this is what you use to feature banner ads for products you are an affiliate of, and are promoting, and also the code to create a sign up box for your mailing list.

Which you will need next... for Quick Tip #4

Quick Tip #4: Start To Build Your List

The next thing I need, to capture the names and emails of all the traffic I'm generating via my blog, my Facebook profile and page, my Twitter timeline and perhaps my YouTube channel, is a mailing list host.

This is an online service, that generates a bit of code, that I can drop into the sidebar of my blog, where folks can give me their name and email in return for a free gift of some kind.

(Don't worry if you don't have one, I'll come back to that in a minute)

How to choose?

The question you have to ask yourself is... 'Am I ever going to want to sell anything of my own - a product, service, workshop, coaching... anything at all?'

If the answer is yes, then you should really look at the service I use, which is TotalBusinessCart. You can start with the basic level and work up to the all-bells-and-whistles version, which offers product management, affiliate management, ad tracking and all sorts.

Everything you need in fact, to run your online business. Enjoy a 30 day trial here, with my best wishes (and yes it is my affiliate link but it won't cost you any more to use it!) http://bit.ly/nctbc

If you never intend to sell anything yourself, but just sell other people's stuff, then you probably only need an email / newsletter service, such as aWeber or GetResponse.

Another reason you might want to use GetResponse for initial contacts is because it has a feature where you can show your prospects a list of other GetResponse ezines (after they have confirmed onto yours!) and you earn credits so that your list gets shown too. This is called co-registration and some people hate it and some people use it in the early days and then stop and some people never go there.

Back to the free gift... if you want to give people something cool for joining your mailing list, there are a number of ways to do that.

You could use one of the free reports from The Money Gym, covering everything from wealth creation to internet marketing.

You could use one of the many ebooks or bits of software that many give away as bonuses with products you may purchase.

You can create your own report or ebook using OpenOffice.org - a bit like Microsoft Word but it's free and the Write part of it has the function of allowing you to turn your written document into a PDF file easily.

Or you could simply interview someone for an hour via a teleconference line, record it, and give the MP3 download away as a gift.

Unique, cheap and a high perceived value to your potential mailing list subscriber.

Quick Tip #5: Set Up A Squeeze Page

The next thing I would do, having already...

1. Set up my email signature with an affiliate link or two.

2. Set up my Facebook page, Twitter account and linked the two.

3. Installed my Wordpress blog onto the 'blog' sub-directory of my new domain name and put a redirect index.php page on the root directory for now. Added content from EzineArticles.com interspersed with unique content.

4. Set up my mailing list host, aWeber initially, for prospects (then Total Business Cart for customers later). See below for links.

Next I would look at setting up a squeeze page as the index page in the root directory - this is where you simply ask for visitors name and email in return for a free gift.

Lots of people hate squeeze pages and refuse to use them but the numbers don't lie.

At the Money Gym, we were converting 1-2% of our traffic to subscribers when we didn't use a squeeze page. As soon as we put one in front of our traffic, we started converting 14% of our visitors to subscribers.

Squeeze pages can be fun, and using video increases your conversions dramatically.

You probably ended up on my mailing list after putting your name and email in a box on my squeeze page.

You use the index page on your main root directory to set up a squeeze page, and you can either make the 'thank you' page your main site or blog, or you can jump people to a page where you educate them about confirming their interest (double opt-in) and then give them the link to your main site in the email they get after confirming their opt-in.

If you feel more comfortable, you can also try out what's called a reverse squeeze page. This is where you give some valuable content first, usually by video, and then encourage people to put their name and email in a box, to get more of the great content.

Quick Tip #6: Learn How To Split Test EVERYTHING

The next thing I would do is learn how to use Google Website Optimizer... *www.google.com/websiteoptimizer*

This is really the one thing I wish I'd learned how to do earlier. Years earlier.

All those millions of variations of the Money Gym website, all those changes, none of them tracked for effectiveness - what a waste of time and effort.

Essentially, if you are using it with a squeeze page, you simply set up an 'experiment' within Google Optimizer, called an A/B Experiment.

Then Google gives you some code - two bits of code which you drop into the source / HTML code of your squeeze page, and then you create a second version of your page with, say, a different headline, and add another bit of code to the source code of that page.

Then you create one 'thank you' page and put a fourth bit of code in the source code of that page.

Then you send all your traffic to your main URL, and Google sends half of it to one version of the page, and half to the other version, and the bit of code on the thank you page tracks which headline was most effective.

Devastatingly simple to use, and you will never have to guess about anything on your site again.

You can split test headlines, or colours of headline, or sub-heads, or calls to action, or the colour of your buy now button...

If you get enough traffic, you can even do something called multi-variate testing. You can test many different versions of your page at once.

Wow!

But be ready for the results - the customers always love the versions you hate!

Can you see how powerful that is? So many people agonise about what to put on their pages... now you don't have to.

Just test and measure, test and measure.

Quick Tip #7: Build A Know, Like & Trust Relationship

The next thing I would do is to decide how I'm going to follow up with subscribers and build a 'know, like & trust' relationship with them.

Because follow up you must!

Even if you hate to write, you need to contact your subscribers ideally every day for a week, then perhaps every 3-4 days for a month, then at least weekly.

The follow up can be largely automated but must be good content and of interest to your 'ideal future customer'. You should also add your follow up to your blog, and think about leverage, if it's unique content, then you can submit it to EzineArticles.com to link back to your new blog.

Talking of EzineArticles.com, you will see if you click through to my Expert Author biography here:
http://ezinearticles.com/?expert_bio=Nicola_Cairncross

I've been a member since 2005 - wow!

I can hardly believe it.

The deal with Ezine Articles.com is that you are allowed to use any article - in a blog, ezine or email - as long as you credit the author, and leave their Author Info and link intact.

There you go, instant content.

Or, if you really want something a bit more special, you could use Martin Avis' brilliant 'Newsletter Success Formula' which you can find out more about here (affiliate link alert) *http://bit.ly/ncmartinavisnsf*

I really rate Martin, he's a successful internet marketer, writes really well, makes most of his money from his regular ezine Kickstart, and has tons of fans.

Martin also runs the London Lunch, for internet marketers to get out from behind their computers and meet each other. Why not come along? Experienced online entrepreneurs rub shoulders with complete newbies and many famous faces turn up when in town. Get on the mailing list for that here: *www.london-lunch.com* (not an affiliate link - I have to pay for my lunch too).

Anyway, if anyone knows how to do automated follow up with a heart it's Martin.

Years before I met Martin, I decided that I wanted to create an automated follow up by email, inspired by the founder of the Coaching movement, Thomas Leonard. I planned out a 101 day series, all around Wealth Creation and started writing. I got to Day 15, and knew that I would never finish unless I had an incentive.

I announced the series on my Google Group (I'd had a box on my little website and many people had joined) and loads of the Google Groupers moved onto my mailing list to get the Wealth Creation tips.

I knew that I only had a 15 days start on the group and that kept me writing the next tip pretty much every day. I'll never forget the day I finished it and thought to myself...

Oh my goodness! I seem to have written enough for an ebook.

So I copied it all into Word and turned it into my first ebook, which sold from my site for a couple of years before I saw Debbie Jenkins from Bookshaker speak and secured a publishing deal with Bookshaker who took my little ebook onto Amazon and into all good bookshops.

You could also write a weekly ezine, like we do, or you could simply write a weekly blog post, rounding up your week, lessons learned, observations made, etc., and then mail out a short message to your list, with a link to your blog post, to keep in touch and bring them back to your blog.

One thing's for sure though, and I want you to PAY ATTENTION!

This is the hurdle at which many people fall. They make the site, set up the list, give away a gift, build a list... but they never bother to follow up regularly.

Shame, because it's really true that the money is in your list.

Whether it's affiliate marketing, selling your own stuff, setting up a membership site, or promoting Joint Venture Partners' products, services or seminars (which gets you in free by the way!) the quality of your relationship with your list is absolutely key to your success online.

That's it - that's my '7 Quick Tips To Build An Online Business If You Don't Have A Real World One' and I really hope you enjoyed them.

But more importantly, I hope you take action on them.

The More Niche The Better

One of the most powerful secrets of the internet is that the more niche your site is, the better. The more esoteric your idea, the more likely you are to attract a faithful following.

I may have told you about my friend who is a successful business travel expert by day, but she creates the most amazing American folk art (Amish style) dolls by night. She buys the patterns and materials direct from the USA, via websites advertising the products. We are trying to persuade her that there may be a market for these dolls via the internet – she currently sells via craft fairs.

So if you have a passion, or a hobby, or something you want to learn about, one of the best ways to make a start is to create a website; you will start to attract people who are interested in the same things as you.

If you then go one step further, and offer a discussion group or newsletter about your chosen subject, you will start to build a reservoir of folk who are on the same wavelength. No matter that you don't yet have a product or service to market to them, you will have a pool of customers or clients for the future, all of whom know other people with the same interests.

If you then think deeply about your chosen subject, especially if it is one that has inspired or affected you deeply, you may be able to come up with five, seven, eight, nine or ten key things that would be useful to other people interested in the same subject. Mindmapping is useful for this exercise.

Perhaps you may choose eight things of interest; for example, Chris who creates the Amish style dolls might choose 'materials', 'patterns', 'history', 'great sites', 'museums', 'experts', 'provenance' and 'regions' then you add the 'discovery/home' page and a 'shop/contact' page, and lo and behold, you have the beginnings of a 10 step e–commerce website, an eprogramme, an ebook, some teleclasses, workshops, or even perhaps a training or coaching programme.

Thomas Leonard, founder of Coachville, created a fantastic eprogramme called 'Passive Revenue for Coaches' which inspired me immensely on this subject; my business coach Chris Barrow perfected the technique of creating a programme (or Gym format) around a coaching speciality and further inspired me.

I have now developed my own 7-Step mentoring program, called 'Hidden Star To Superstar' to take anyone or any business online, following the exact process I used to build The Money Gym from zero to a six-figure plus turnover online, in just 3 years.

ACTION STEP

Pick A Subject, Any Subject.

What do you know about, are passionate about, have experienced or have skills in?

Who might want what you know? Who might want to learn your skills? Who might need the resources you have gathered? Who might be going through the same experiences as you?

If you create a community, post up links, start to build a reservoir of people and then eventually you will come up with a range of affordable and more top of the range products or services with which to serve that community.

As I have said, in the words of Napoleon Hill in 'Think & Grow Rich', if you can find a way to serve the greatest number of people then the river of abundance will flow for you. I like that idea. Serve people and benefit. And the internet is the best way that I know of to serve the most number of people almost effortlessly.

Business Is All About Making Sales!

When you first go into business, either on- or off-line, in order to make successful sales, you need to ask yourself some crucial questions:

Who is your IDEAL customer?

By which I mean the person who has a burning pain or problem, that your product or service solves or soothes. They must also be able to afford your product or service. What do they look like, how do they make their money, how do they live their lives, what do they do in their spare time?

Where are you going to find your customers?

If you have answered the question about the ideal customer fully, you should have a pretty good idea of where you will be able to find them, but I want you to think specifically where they hang out online. You can reach a great number of people online, whereas if you limit your customer base to your home town... well, it's not going to be so profitable.

If you think that your ideal customer will be hanging out on Google, looking for a solution to their problem or pain, that's the first place for you to look too.

Use the Google Keyword tool:
https://adwords.google.co.uk/select/KeywordToolExternal

People either search by the problem or pain, or their perceived solution to the problem or pain.

For example: I've got bad spots (keyword 'spots' or 'bad spots') or 'how can I get rid of my spots' or 'fast spot relief' (new keyword 'spot relief' or 'fast spot relief').

Google will tell you how many of your ideal customers are searching for you right now per month, globally and locally, and what words they are using, specifically, to search with. You might find that quite motivating!

What product will you sell them first?

So, by looking at the phrases that are getting the most searches per month, globally or nationally, you will be able to think of things to sell them – and the first one of those is your lead product.

You might have a few free products to give away first, but the important one is the first paid product.

Michael Masterson, in his superb business book 'Ready Fire Aim' says that 'until you have a lead product that you can sell profitably, to your ideal customer, you don't have a business.'

How much will you charge them for it?

This is an easy one to answer – you test three different price points, and you do that using a simple bit of code, that fires one third of your customers at one sales page, with a price at X, the second third at a second page with a price at Y, and the final third at a third page with a price point of Z.

How will you convince them to buy it?

Now, this is getting a little more complex, but once you know the elements of a sale, you will do very well.

First up, you will need a long-form sales page – and before you groan and say you hate them... we have all tested them and they sell the most so GET OVER IT.

I use Armand Morin's Sales Letter Generator to write mine, then I give it to Steve to pretty it up and get it online, then we link to it from emails, from our website, in our ezine.

The sections of the long-form sales page are covered, in logical step by step sequence, in the Sales Letter Generator tool, but the most important elements are:

- **Social Proof** – this means testimonials from happy customers – video and pictures prove that they are real people and if some of them are well known so much the better!
- **Proof** - this means specific proof that your product or services does what you say it does.
- **Reciprocity** – If you do something for someone else, like give them lots of great free stuff, they tend to want to do something for you. It's human nature to want to return the favour.
- **Risk Reversal** – this is your crucially important guarantee and it needs to take all the risk away from the customer and put it onto you.
- **Urgency** – people need a reason to buy now or they will never make a decision.

What Next?

As I did when I planned out my 101 eprogramme, you could plan out how you are going to deliver your knowledge or expertise.

So you have your seven, eight, nine or ten key topics. Let's say ten (I like round numbers!). You have started to build your community of people who are interested in the subject at hand. What next?

Add recommended reading for each of the 10 key topics, a useful exercise, links to great websites related to the key topics. Can you see how you are starting to build something of real worth?

But as the previous section covered, you need to work out what you are going to sell and how much you are going to charge for it.

The first thing is to decide if you are going to sell to a global market (advised!) or your local market as that will decide which currency you set up your shopping cart in.

It's a well known fact that, if you don't sell in dollars, you won't sell as much to the American market and they are still one of the biggest markets buying online, although there are more people in China on broadband right now (2010) than there are alive in the entire USA!

The next thing to do is to develop three ways for people to experience your programme. Three different price points with the middle one being your ideal scenario.

You could create an eprogramme (essentially an eBook, chunked down into the 10 topics, and then further into 3, 5, or 10 key points on each topic). eProgrammes are delivered via autoresponders. My Money Gym book started life as a Financial Intelligence eBook & Work Programme, broken down into 10 key topics (or modules or chapters) then chunked down into the 101 day eprogramme this book is based upon.

At the time of writing originally, this book is actually my lowest price point at the moment. Since then we have added many other different price point 'lead products' all of which encourage people to join the membership site.

Your eprogramme/eBook can be purchased by visitors through a shopping cart on your website (as I mentioned in the Quick Tips, I use TotalBusinessCart.com which is a great product and delivers everything you need – a one stop marketing and delivery solution). You could charge anything between £17.95 and £79.95 for the eBook and especially if you bundle it up into an ebook / audio / video package.

Interestingly for a long time, most people ended up choosing the highest level coaching option at The Money Gym which goes against popular pricing wisdom (possibly because I personally believe it delivers the most value and the most effective coaching combination and I obviously subconsciously put this over when talking to people).

You could start with an eprogramme, build that into an ebook, then offer a top of the range option including email support from you as they work through the materials. Or perhaps your top of the range option is workshops. Or 1–to–1 coaching.

But remember as you consider this option, the more 1–to–1 time you spend, the fewer clients you can serve and the more limits you put on your income. Always remember the ideal of creating passive income flows. This dictates that you should try and set your options up to be able to serve the most number of people at any time.

Are you starting to think that this could be fun?

ACTION STEP

Draw a circle on a piece of paper. Draw 10 little lines coming out from the circle. Draw 10 circles at the end of each line.

Draw 10 little lines coming out from each of these circles with little circles at the end of each. This is your programme outline. All you have to do now is fill up all of the circles and you will have created your programme. Choose a smaller number than 10 if you are struggling to fill the circles.

Now think about your three price points and product progressions.

Add one book recommendation for each of the 10 main circles, one website resource and one exercise that you feel would be the most helpful to illustrate the topic covered.

We are nearly there now.

THE MONEY GYM WORKOUT PLAN

These are the actions I will take in the next month, arising from Module 8: Profit from Your Passion

1. _____
2. _____
3. _____
4. _____
5. _____
6. _____
7. _____
8. _____
9. _____
10. _____
11. _____
12. _____
13. _____
14. _____
15. _____
16. _____
17. _____
18. _____
19. _____
20. _____

Signed: _____ Date: _____

MODULE 9

Mind Your Own 'Real World' Business

When I started my first ever business at the age of 8 years old, I accidentally did something totally wrong and something totally right.

It was my idea to rent out, or even sell, the many paperback story books I had already accumulated from older relatives, second hand shops and jumble sales.

I started well, planning out how to keep track of who had borrowed which book (modelled on the already successful methods employed by my local library – why re-invent the wheel?) and I'd gathered all the necessary equipment, including a John Bull's Printing Kit to date stamp the books, albeit a touch on the slow side, due to having to manually change the numbers each day!

We even had premises, the 'under the stairs cupboard' was requisitioned, in spite of my fear of the feather duster, but this was not my main concern because I had already decided I wasn't going to man the shop, my trusty assistant Heather was!

O yes! One of my more clever moves was that I recruited my 6-year old sister, Heather (now an international opera singer and still dining out on the story!) on a payment-by-results basis and the plan was that I was going to go out around the local playgrounds marketing my new book-lending business, while Heather waited patiently under the stairs, reading the merchandise in order to better demonstrate the pleasure to be gained from any loan or purchase.

One of my LEAST clever moves was not doing any market research, particularly NOT finding out whether there was a ravenging, hungry horde of kids looking for my solution to their problem or challenge.

Because there wasn't.

I was the only asthmatic, fairytale crazy, reading-mad child locally – the rest were very busy having fun outdoors and they wanted to read LESS not more!

Oh dear. Duh! Double Duh In Marketing Terms!

I'm sorry to say that this was only the first of many, many businesses that I started on a whim, on the back of a good idea, that I got going BEFORE I tested the market or found out if there was a demand.

At the Money Gym, we firmly believe that setting up a part time business (NOT a part time job, note!) can be one of the easiest, quickest first steps you can take in increasing your income but we want you to do it right!

Why Start A Business At All?

We have covered the tax advantages of starting a business alongside your day job in previous modules but it does bear repeating.

Especially if you start a business around a passion, it will often mean that any training, research materials (including magazines), conferences in far flung places, travel to and from meetings with potential strategic partners, etc, can be legitimate tax deductible expenses.

You can also often claim for things like mobile phones, travel, cars, home telephones, a proportion of your mortgage interest, light, heat and water, as well as a certain amount of office furniture and equipment.

You need to get specialist advice on this from your accountant, of course, but you may be amazed.

What you don't want to happen however, is to ruin something that you love by turning it into a job. You must design it for success from Day 1, and don't ever be tricked into thinking that because you are doing it in your spare time, you should be anything less than professional and business–like.

Or you could end up giving up your day job (and that horrible boss) for a job with longer hours, even less job security and an even worse boss – you!

However, there is a saying that you won't ever be free until you look in the mirror in the morning and the boss is looking back at you.

ACTION STEP

Why do you want to start a business? If it's just to escape from a job you hate, then think again.

How much training do you have to run a business? If none, don't despair – you can teach yourself to be a business person.

Start by reading 'The E–Myth Revisited' by Michael E Gerber and/or visiting the website at www.emyth.com. It's possibly the finest book on the planet about starting and running a successful business.

Work, Rest & Play

I'll never forget my first day at Art College. I had worked for six years before joining my local college as a mature student on the Fashion Design course. I had been taken in on the strength of my ability to design in my head and translate that into patterns and actual clothes. I could barely draw and had no portfolio, neither had I done the required foundation course. They said I would have to work extra hard.

I came to college from working as an ad sales rep, a clerical officer at Southern Water Authority, a hairdresser... all sorts of horrible jobs I hated.

The first lesson on the first day at Art College was about... well, I have no idea what it was about!

We were told to spend the next three days creating a sculpture out of rubbish that we collected ourselves. My new friend and I wandered about Worthing, collecting the most interesting and esoteric bits of rubbish we could find, until we had created a pretentious Heath Robinson–like contraption that had to be displayed in a cupboard because it lit up like a beacon and twinkled with chrome and various spangly bits and candles.

I remember thinking this isn't work, this is playing! It's like being back at kindergarten or nursery school. And so it went on, with each day becoming more and more enjoyable and the days racing past – until the day came to write my dissertation but that's another story.

The point of this story is to reflect on the fact that, when you are doing something you love, where you can be creative, where you are not tied to an office from 8am to 6pm and are free to set your own hours, the time races past and hardly anything seems to be a chore.

But actually, this is when you need to be at your most grown–up. As you move from the left hand side of the cashflow quadrant to the right, from an employee (toddler) to a self employed person (teenager), to a Business Person (grown–up) to an Investor (wise elder of the tribe) you must become more responsible, not less.

Responsible to whom? Why, to you, of course! Because as you move from the perceived security of a job, into the apparent freedom of self employment, through to being responsible for the direction of your own company (and other people's jobs) through to being responsible for your own money, you must grow, evolve and learn new skills all the time.

But if you don't find the idea of evolving, learning and growing, exciting and challenging, then skip this module. Because you will turn something you love (a hobby, interest or enjoyment) into a disaster waiting to happen. And you will spoil for yourself the very thing that inspired you to start in the first place.

However, if you find the idea of evolving, learning and growing, exciting and challenging. And the idea of creating a business from a passion you hold is attractive to you, then life can indeed become very wonderful. Almost as wonderful as it seemed when you were a kid and just knew that you could become anything you wanted to be.

ACTION STEP

Remember When You Were Eight

One of the things I ask my clients to think about when working through this module on a 1-to-1 basis, is what they enjoyed doing when they were eight years old. What did you get so absorbed in, that you lost track of time. What were your passions then?

List them down and try to add to them while you work through this module.

What did you daydream about?

Look In The Mirror... Who Do You See?

One of the main reasons people start to consider turning a hobby or interest into a business or income flow is because they want to be set free from their job.

'The E-Myth Revisited' by Michael E Gerber covers this topic in great detail, but you must consider the possibility that the very thing you love doing, if not set up properly, could turn into a job of the worst kind; long hours, no security and no steady income flow. What a tragedy that would be.

But if you set things up properly, so that your fledgling business will, one day, be able to function without you, then your passion could turn into an extra stream of income, or even better, a passive income flow. This can work if you develop a team of people to actually do the time consuming work, or if you take your new business online, automating many of the functions usually performed by people.

If you get it right, you will have ultimate control, not only over your new business (which you can run from anywhere in the world, even a beach in Greece) but over your life. If your little sideline develops to the stage where the income overtakes that of your day job, then you will be set free.

No-one will ever be able to tell you what to do again, unless you choose to give them that power. Interestingly, and ironically, many people find that they start to love their job again as soon as they know that they could walk away if they chose to!

How would it feel to know that no–one will be able to take away your (or your family's) security, by making you redundant? You will never have to worry about retirement because your business will continue to generate an income flow on an ongoing basis.

The reason I am so keen to encourage my clients to develop a little business based on a hobby or passion, is that it takes some effort to turn the TV off and take some action. It's a lot easier to raise the enthusiasm if you are interested in the subject in the first place.

If you spend a lot of time doing something anyway, it's not such a leap to make, to turn it into an income stream.

ACTION STEP

What Do You Do In The Evenings?

What do you spend most of your leisure time doing? Wide ranging hobbies that could be developed include wine tasting, cooking, cross–stitch, reading science fiction (particularly feminist science fiction!), American folk crafts & embroidery, fly–fishing, kick–boxing, genealogy, ghost–hunting, complementary therapies, cameo painting, watercolour & life drawing, looking at properties, DIY, growing medieval organic herbs, etc.

Funnily enough, the more obscure and specialist the passion, the easier it is to make money from it online.

A good way to research how many people are looking for things to buy online, is to visit the Google KeyWord Tool at: *https://adwords.google.co.uk/select/KeywordToolExternal*

And type in anything you can think of. You will see immediately how many thousands of people are searching the internet for that key word or phrase. You can search by UK or USA only, or get the Global search numbers.

Nicola's Theory of Evolution

One of the most powerful quotes I have come across is from one of the interviewees in the 'Conversations With Millionaires' book by Mike Litman. It says 'One of the most powerful reasons to set a goal to become a millionaire is because of the things you will learn along the way'.

I actually left school as a delinquent under–achiever, who scraped five 'O' Levels but could have done so much better. Always in the A stream (by the skin of my teeth and sheer force of my charm I always think!)

but always hanging out behind the bike sheds with the smokers and the bad boys and girls. No college, no sixth–form, no idea of what to do.

I have jumped from job to job, always searching for the 'one'; the job where I would shine, show my true potential, where I would fulfil the potential I knew was there, where I wouldn't be bored stiff. I had one job that was so boring that I used to go and cry in the loos. Then I moved from one start up business to the next, always searching for my big break. No training (beyond the very perfunctory), no business skills, no idea. I wasn't sorry for myself because I didn't know there was anything better.

However, I was a voracious reader and in between the horror and sci–fi stories, I occasionally bought a 'self–help' book such as 'How To Become A Woman of Substance' and 'How To Love A Difficult Man'. Oh, how my husband laughed when he found that one. Little did he know that I bought it when we started going out together! I've needed it a few times since too!

But I digress!

I then discovered personal development and coaching, simultaneously. The missing piece of the puzzle turned out to be actually doing the exercises at the end of the chapters! It took a year of coaching to get me there but the worm turned with a vengeance then.

So, since this turning–point, I have crammed a lifetime of missed learning into my head. I go to conferences and seminars, I read personal development and business books before I go to sleep at night and I attend teleclasses, workshops and conferences. I have a business coach, a technology coach and I have been in therapy for nearly five years, dealing with the self–esteem issues that come from growing up with a mother challenged with mental illness.

I can't get enough learning – I'm hungry for it – especially about what was once the most challenging subject of all for me – making and keeping money.

Creating abundance for myself, my family, my clients and my preferred causes. And it turns out that one of my four core needs is learning.

I can't function without learning something new, being in a state of mental growth. Intriguingly, one of my four core values is also learning. It gives me joy, makes my soul fly, gives me hope and light.

It's the journey, not the destination. The process, not the outcome.

The ability to pass on what I learn so that if just one person does not have to struggle like I did, then I will have achieved more than I ever dreamed of at school.

And I am privileged to be able to profit from my passion.

ACTION STEP

What makes your soul fly? What sets you on fire? How can you take the advice of Napoleon Hill in 'Think & Grow Rich' when he says something along the lines of 'if you can find a way to serve the greatest number of people, then the river of abundance will flow for you'.

What would you really like to learn more about?

Much more?

Because that could be the key to your online riches – if you learn about something and share what you are learning, via a blog, you will attract a community of people who know who you are, and what you know.

And you might find a way to serve them, by sharing what you are learning.

Zest For Life

One of my clients said to me the other day, 'Nicola, I was awake at the crack of dawn – I just couldn't sleep! I woke up so excited and fired up, I just had to get up and start.'

When Gill and I started The Wealth Company, we would often find emails from each other sent at 5am, 6am, 7am, and this was a Saturday morning! She would send me an email expecting to have to wait till 10am or so for an answer, but get one back immediately. We nicknamed our company 'Nighties R Us' because we would sneak downstairs while the kids were asleep and get some work done – not because we had to, but because it was fun!

When asked about my hobbies, I have to confess, while I still have an interest in feminist science fiction, cooking, nu–soul music, holidays in Greece and many other things, I would have to count personal and financial development among them now.

Working on something you love blurs the line between work and play. You have to be very careful not to tip over into workaholic mode.

Where does the line between loving what you do, and being unable to stop, begin and end?

But I bet you must be dying to get going by now? However, the thing that holds most people back is wondering what they can do. They think that they don't know enough, need more skills, knowledge, experience and equipment perhaps.

I don't agree. The process or journey is the thing and the learning is the thing.

I think that everyone has a hobby or interest that can be turned into a business and that, if you just start, you may very well not end up where you imagined, but you will end up somewhere different and that 'somewhere different' will be better and further along than where you are now.

What do you feel passionate about, what life experiences have you had, what specialist knowledge do you have access to, that people might want enough to pay for?

Have you ever felt pain, either mental or physical? How did you get through it? Have you ever overcome a difficult situation? How did you cope? What resources did you research? What phone numbers, email addresses, websites do you know about that really helped you?

Have you had a baby, cared for elderly or sick relatives, started a business, been a mature student, got out of debt, married someone from a different race or faith?

Someone, somewhere, out there is going through the same experiences you have. What would have helped you then? What would have been useful to you?

And perhaps they would pay, just a little, for that support, information or resource.

ACTION STEP

One of the first things I do with my internet marketing mentoring clients, while working through our 'Hidden Star To Superstar' program, is to use mindmapping to plan out an online learning package, that could be sold as an information product online.

If you can draw a circle in the middle of a sheet of paper and put in a working title for your program, then draw 7-10 other bubbles around it.

Fill those in with the 7-10 things you think people need to know, about your main topic.

For example, each chapter in this book originally started life as one of my 10 bubbles.

Then I added one or two books that people ought to read, to deepen their understanding of that particular topic.

Then I added one or two websites they ought to visit, and any other resources I could think of, such as useful exercises they could do.

Effortless Attraction

When you first start out on your road to Financial Intelligence, it may seem as if you are surrounded by negativity and nay–sayers. Everyone will have a good reason why it will not work, bad stories about people they know, tips from the newspapers about what you shouldn't get involved in. Often these 'warnings' will be your friends and family. These people always have your 'best interests' at heart so don't get mad.

As Anita Roddick once said, 'Keep your dream to yourself until it comes true.' I always like to think of my dreams as fragile little creatures, that you will hold close to your heart and safe, but gently. Don't grip too tightly or expose it to the elements too soon.

Telling people what you want to do – whether it's becoming financially free or starting a new business – is exposing your dreams to the elements. Not getting started, or being too secretive, is gripping too tightly. But as you go along your path, you will notice that you are getting to know new people.

You will become friends with people who have similar interests to you; the right kind of people to support and encourage you. I became very friendly with my dentist, Ross. Ross is a property and equities investor as well as a dentist and I actually look forward to going to the dentist now as we try and swap stories on my wealth creation activities and his – no easy feat with a bunch of hands and shiny instruments in my mouth, I can tell you.

I now often meet new friends at the training seminars I attend and the conferences I am invited to speak at. I also often become quite close friends with ex–clients, once they have achieved their financial goals and moved on a bit. They go on to other mentors and we become friends.

As you become more positive, confident and sure of yourself, you will become more attractive to positive, confident, outgoing, open–minded people. You will become a magnet for people who are doing the same things you are doing. People will come up to you to talk and you will never be afraid of being in a room of strangers again – because you will know that each of those strangers will have something of value to teach you.

Thomas Leonard, founder of the coaching movement, used to use the term 'effortless attraction' to describe the principle, that the more you work on yourself, your personal growth and your own activities, the more you will attract the people who will want to help and support you. It works even better if you become more self–ish, as Thomas called it. Becoming aware of the environments you need to flourish; environments include the people around you.

I notice this happening more and more in my own life and it's a joy. I used to work in the music industry which was terrible for 'posers, liggers and hangers–on' as they were known. And everyone was very affected by the clothes people wore, the music they liked and the useful people they knew.

I used to hate the word 'network' because it had such horrid connotations. Now I know that 'network' means 'meet new friends' I am constantly amazed and delighted by the wonderful kinds of people who are attracted to me nowadays, both new friends and clients.

ACTION STEP

Laura Berman Fortgang's business coaching book 'Take Yourself To The Top' has a brilliant chapter on building meaningful business relationships and I have found it works just as well for personal relationships too.

It encourages you to sort out your friends, family and contacts into your 'Inside 10' and your 'Top 20'. The Inside 10 are the people you want to keep in touch with at least weekly and the Top 20 are those who you want to keep in contact with monthly.

Then you imagine yourself picking up the phone to each one and you notice how your body responds at the thought. Does your heart lift or your stomach sink at the thought of calling that person?

If the latter, then cross them off your list – no matter how influential, useful or well–connected. If the former, then keep them there.

Don't worry if you don't have a full list to start with. It will be fun filling it up!

Designing For Success

So many people start a new business by planning it to work (or not) on a shoestring.

They work out the minimum they can spend on marketing, don't imagine that they will need any staff, muddle through without a business plan, then wonder where all their money has gone.

After many years of start–up struggle I came across a fairly revolutionary idea in the seminal business book 'The E–Myth Revisited' by Michael E Gerber. You are going to hear a lot about this book in this module!

Remember I was a serial entrepreneur, had attended a lot of business startup training seminars. I knew all the statistics about 80% of all new businesses failing in the first year and something like 50% of the other 20% failing over the next three years.

I really thought I knew it all about starting up new businesses. I even earned a living starting up businesses for other people. I really thought success in business was about keepin' on keepin' it on, just keep trying different ideas until you hit pay dirt. Remember that this was the time of the dot com boom, when entrepreneurs were at last being taken seriously in the UK, which was radical enough in itself.

The idea Michael Gerber was putting forward was that you should design a business for success from Day 1.

Radical stuff. Assume that a new business was going to succeed and put the systems in place accordingly? Outrageous! This was only the first radical concept in that book but I'll go into the others in later segments.

So what does it mean to design a business for success? You are just about to find out in this module.

ACTION STEP

Designing Your Business For Success

Look at your existing business for a moment. What would you do differently if you could be absolutely certain that your business was going to go stratospheric?

What systems would you put in place, who would you recruit, what board of directors would you find, what training would you get?

Another great book to read is Michael Masterson's 'Ready, Fire Aim' which is one of the best business books I've ever read.

The Curse of The Entrepreneur

The major challenge faced by many of my clients is that of having too many ideas. When I created this module 'Profit From Your Passion' I fondly imagined that people would say that they didn't have anything of interest to work on, they didn't have any interesting hobbies, no skills and no passions that could be turned into income flows.

I was ready with a whole string of ideas and exercises to stimulate creativity but in the end, how wrong I was!

Happily, I have attracted raging entrepreneurs who have the other challenge – too many ideas. The trouble with entrepreneurs is that they think that they have to act on each idea immediately, that a good idea will slip away if not 'worked up' and then, several days later when the first flush of enthusiasm wears off, or the first hurdle is reached, the entrepreneur goes off the whole idea.

This leads to their being branded a 'flake', or as someone who can't stick at anything for 'long enough'.

I'll never forget my first coach, Rachel Turner, saying to me that I shouldn't ever worry about having to act on every idea immediately, that the flow of ideas would never dry up. She recommended a treasure box where you make a note of each idea (on the assumption that a good idea will still be a good idea next week or the week after) and this enables you to carry on working on the current idea without distraction.

About the same time, an entrepreneur and employer of mine told me that, when he had a new idea, he deliberately sat on it for a whole week, then, on the Sunday after he had the idea, he made a decision as to whether to pursue it.

And around that time I started my coach training, where super–coach and raging entrepreneur Thomas Leonard came into my life. His take on this was that it was OK to work on more than one thing at a time, as long as each thing you were working on synergised with the others.

For a while I found it hard to reconcile the three things I wanted to work on with this principle, even though the sense of it rang true. A coaching practice, a hotel and a music industry website? Join the dots on that one! I never even mentioned each of them on the other websites.

Then I realised that, for a wealth creation coach specialising in enabling people to create a business (the hotel), passive income online (the music industry website), and continuous personal and financial development (wealth coaching), each activity added credibility to my coaching, because I was actually working on all of the things I was recommending.

Voila! Synergy in motion.

ACTION STEP

In an ideal life, what are the three things you would most like to work on, right now, all at once?

If anything else crops up then write the idea down and put it in your treasure box for later.

Draw three circles on a piece of paper, write each idea in a circle, then draw little lines coming out of each circle and create more circles at the end of the lines. Write down the qualities or elements or benefits of each idea in the new circles. Now study each in turn – do they have any sub–circles in common? Draw lines connecting them, if they do.

This is a process I call Synergy Mapping and, for creative people, it is the best way to get ideas and information out of their heads, and into a place where they can start to organise it and make connections.

If you can make any connections between the three things, then you can start to see where the synergy may lie and you have my full permission <grin> to go for it!

Technicians, Managers & Entrepreneurs

Michael Gerber, author of 'E–Myth Revisited' has identified three distinct personality types in business; the Entrepreneur, the Manager and the Technician, but before we go there, I would like to share his thinking about the idea that your business is nothing more than a distinct reflection of who you are.

He argues that, if you are sloppy, your business will be sloppy. If you are disorganised, then your business will be disorganised. If you are greedy, then your employees will be greedy, giving you less and less of themselves and always asking for more. Why not look deep inside yourself and if you have a business already, see if you can identify some of your personality traits in your business' personality. What do you see?

Furthermore, he asserts that the first fundamental change that has to take place, has to do with your idea of what a business really is and what it takes to make one work.

Michael says that most businesses are started by Technicians having an entrepreneurial seizure. And that they make a Fatal Assumption, and it is that if you understand the technical work of a business, you understand a business that does technical work.

It just isn't true. The technical work of a business and a business that does that technical work are two totally different things. What mostly happens with startups is that Technicians take the work they love and turn it into a job. Born out of love and a pride in their workmanship, it becomes a chore. They experience exhilaration, terror, exhaustion and finally, despair. This is where the high failure rate of start up businesses kicks in.

Yet still, barbers open barber shops, graphic designers open graphic design companies, musicians open musical shops, engineers open semi–conductor businesses, ex–marketing directors open marketing consultancies. And, rather than being their greatest asset, their technical knowledge becomes their greatest liability.

But I'm getting ahead of myself here. And I want to reassure you that I am a very positive person and I believe with all my heart that starting a business, even alongside your job perhaps, is one of the four great ways to become financially free. The good news is that you can learn how to create a successful business, no matter which personality type you are.

The Entrepreneur sees exceptional opportunities, they are visionaries and dreamers, energetic and motivated. Living in the future, never in the past, rarely in the present. Usually with a strong need for control and change.

The Manager is pragmatic and lives in the past. Highly organised and craving order. Clinging to the status quo and seeing the obstacles and problems.

The Technician is the 'do–er'. They like to do things right and do it themselves. Living in the present and loving the feel of things. Happy working but only on one thing at a time. The backbone of every culture but only producing bread for tonight's table.

The Entrepreneur dreams, the Manager worries and the Technician ruminates. But the fact of the matter is that we all have a bit of each in us, while our personalities are dominated by one most of the time. I'm an Entrepreneur, for the record!

Furthermore, each business goes through three distinct phases. The startup, infancy or Technician phase, then the adolescence, survival or Manager phase when you need to get some help, then the Mature or Entrepreneurial phase. But you have to pass beyond the owner's comfort zone before you can get there, and that is another danger zone.

Imagine a successful business as a bunch of people going on a car trip. The Entrepreneur is the one standing up, head out of the sunroof, eyes fixed on the horizon, with a very clear vision of where the business is going. The Manager makes sure there are car rugs, sandwiches, money for petrol and maps. The Technician has already checked the tyres, petrol, moving parts and has the toolkit ready in case the car breaks down. All are equally necessary for a successful outcome to the journey.

ACTION STEP

Every successful business needs contributions from each personality type. So it's important for you to recognise your type and put a team around you to provide the bits you are missing. If you are a Technician you won't be happy managing and will never do the strategic thinking necessary for a long term business success. If you are an Entrepreneur you will need a Manager to get things organised and a Technician to actually do them. If you are a Manager, then you will need to work with an Entrepreneur (perhaps in the form of a non-executive director) and a Technician.

Decide on your type and then think about the people you could work with, or use as consultants, or co–opt onto your virtual Board of Directors, who would fill the other roles. Organise a meeting to discuss your types and how your roles could be adapted to suit your type. Perhaps a Dream Team made up of the three personality types, who meet regularly would give you balanced feedback?

Once you come clean and admit your type, you will stop trying to fit your square peg into a round hole and use all your energy instead to make your business a success.

The Franchise Prototype

Gerber goes on to describe the phenomenon of the Franchise Prototype or the Turnkey Operation. If you set up your business from Day One so that anyone – even a sixteen year old with half a brain – could walk in and follow the procedures, then you are nearly there, in creating a business that does not depend on you to succeed. This is the McDonalds model. No matter what your thoughts about fast food, or burgers, or McDonalds' burgers, they are delivering a product that you can rely on to be consistent, country by country, branch by branch, every single day.

And isn't that what we would all like? The successful business that makes you money regardless of whether you are there, working in the business rather than on the business?

Interestingly enough, it is exactly the opposite to the kind of business you are encouraged to start if you visit one of the high street banks or the numerous government agencies that exist to help small business startups, useful though these organisations are.

When I bought my boutique hotel, The Acacia, everyone thought I was mad to put a manager in there at the beginning. But I knew that I wanted to create a turnkey operation and yes, while I did make mistakes, it was not the concept of having the manager that was wrong.

Personal circumstances then dictated that I worked in the business for a year but I always had the intention that, when the right person came along, I would snap them up. It was hard to look for someone, because I was so busy working in the business (cooking the breakfasts, supervising the cleaners, taking bookings, etc), that I still did not work *on* the business. No marketing to speak of, no strategic planning, no looking ahead. Far too busy for any of that.

It was only when my favourite restaurant went on the market and the manager was facing redundancy that I was handed a golden opportunity to employ a manager to run the business my way, on a day to day basis, while I get on with working on the business rather than in it. Then my Dad offered to move into The Acacia while my family and I took our first holiday for years, and suddenly I realised that the hotel would be better run by someone else – preferably someone not doing three different work things; coaching, internet entrepreneuring, hoteliering while trying to be a mum.

Dad's arrival, and the imminent arrival of Steve Watson, the new manager, also necessitated my writing the Systems Manual, or as I prefer to call it, the 'How We Do It Here' manual. When I was working in the business we didn't need a systems manual because I knew how to do things. Lord knows what would have happened if I'd had an accident or been taken ill!

But Dad needed a 'see at a glance' book that he could refer to and so I finally got around to writing it. I'm a very visual person so I used a mind–map first to organise the information, then with one click of a button I converted it into a powerpoint presentation that could be printed off, and amended every time we changed things.

Once you have written down 'How You Do It Here' you have started to create a Franchise Prototype. If you create a successful business, documented as to how you make it a success, you have a business that someone else could buy, walk in and run (a turnkey operation in other words), or copy (paying you a license fee of course) or even one that you could turn into a book or a programme that could be sold online to other people who want to create a business just like yours.

Now that's an exciting idea, isn't it?

ACTION STEP

To start to create a 'How We Do It Here' manual, just take some paper and draw a circle with the name of your business inside. Even if you are only thinking of starting a business, this can be a useful way to start that business plan you have been putting off. Create little balloons coming off the central circle with the main parts of your business listed inside those balloons.

Then take just one of those balloons and look at it. Create more balloons coming off it, with the next level of information about that part of your business. For example, my first level hotel balloons were 'manager's daily responsibilities', 'manager's weekly responsibilities' and 'manager's quarterly responsibilities'. On the first level of the 'daily responsibilities' there were new balloons saying 'breakfast', 'supervising cleaning' and 'security' among others. Under 'breakfast' there was another level that said things like 'kitchen' and 'dining room'. Under 'dining room' there was 'laying tables', 'making coffee' and 'music'. Under 'music' there was instructions on how to work the hi–fi so that the classical music we play comes through the speakers into the dining room. And what kind of music to play, and which albums are preferred.

And that's just one example of 'How We Do It' at The Acacia. The other benefit is, when I walk into the dining room and find soft rock playing, I can point to the manual and say, 'that's *not* how we do it here,' and there is no room for negotiation, error or mistake, because it's all been spelled out in advance. People know what you expect of them.

How much easier does that make managing people?

Working *On* Your Business

When I first started living and working at the hotel, I used to cook the breakfasts. I was working *in* the business. I actually enjoyed it (apart from getting up early) and then I found a wonderful cleaner called Gianna, who used to arrive at ten past nine, just as I finished breakfast. I used to walk out of the kitchen, she would walk in and start to clear up after me. She would then go on to clean and refresh the rooms.

Usually in a hotel, the breakfast chef would also clear the kitchen (unless they had under–chefs) but I started my 'day job' of coaching at 10am and needed to prepare for my first call. I was working *in* my coaching business.

I had problems with my head on Mondays and Fridays though, because I didn't coach (working in my coaching business) by telephone on those days, so had no good reason not to clean the kitchen (working in my hotel business) or the rooms. I almost felt guilty because I wasn't in there, getting my hands dirty, doing some work. As Gianna hoovered around me, I used to imagine that she was thinking, 'who does she think she is, pretending to work on that computer or going out to meetings all the time, while I do the real work here'. I'm sure she didn't think those thoughts – or if she did, she didn't say them out loud – but that was the kind of dialogue that my 'gremlin voice' was running through my head.

But I pushed through the discomfort because I had read, 'E–Myth Revisited' and I still asked Gianna to work on Mondays and Fridays because those were the days that I set aside to work *on* my various businesses. The days I would look at my admin, finance and marketing, meet inspiring people (and my bank manager) and dream and plan for the future.

On Mondays, particularly, I used to meet my sister for a couple of hours and we would look at what had been better about the previous week, what would have to happen in the forthcoming week for us to be able to look back and say, 'yes! That was better' and what we would need to do, this week, for that to happen. Working on our different businesses, together. We used to do that at a cafe overlooking the sea and most people would have looked at us and thought 'coffee and gossip' but we knew better.

How many times have you thought that you would like to put together a new marketing plan, take some time to revisit your business plan, have regular meetings with inspiring mentors, go to a networking meeting, get some training, write your Systems Manual, visit a competitor or do one of the many very important (rather than urgent) things to move your business forward? And how many times have you put it off, saying to yourself that you are just too busy. Busy doing *very urgent* things. There are always urgent things to do, rather than doing the important things, as Stephen Covey says in '7 Habits of Highly Effective People'. How do you differentiate? Ask yourself, 'will this improve my business or move it forward?' Or perhaps, 'is this an income generating activity?' If not, it's urgent but not important.

A very inspirational book on this topic is 'The One Minute Manager' by Ken Blanchard. He talks about the great manager as someone who always has an empty desk, an open door, who can respond to situations or crisis in seconds because he always has space in his diary, who can spend time thinking about how to make things better.

The great manager always has time because he has effectively delegated all the non–important work; he concentrates only on the important things. But so many people get their sense of worth from being busy. The more *busy* you are, the harder you are working, the more important you feel, the more you are worth, right? No! Wrong, wrong, wrong!

You know you are getting there on this issue when you go into work or your home office, and don't yet know what you will be doing all day. It almost sounds boring, doesn't it? The other way you will know that you are getting there is when you quite happily schedule time in your diary to just *think* about things. Several hours in fact. Or you can schedule time to read that latest business or management book. Or you have nothing scheduled in your diary at all.

How scary is that thought, right now?

ACTION STEP

Look at your diary. Do you have a great long 'to do' list? Is your diary chock a block? You need to be ruthless here and go through your diary or 'to do' list and ask yourself, is this important to my business, or just urgent?

How can you delegate the urgent, while leaving yourself free to concentrate on the important stuff?

And how does that idea make you feel?

Raising Finance

This module is not about the many different kinds of finance available for businesses or how to go about it. Your bank manager, accountant or any good business book can tell you that. It's about the many misconceptions that aspiring entrepreneurs have around the whole concept of new business finance and how to avoid making some basic mistakes. How do I know? Because I made them all! So hopefully this module will get your head into the right place to look at the finance issue with more clarity.

Okay, so raising finance for a new business. What does it really mean?

Once my clients grasp the importance of starting a business in their wealth creation plan, once they have had their great business idea, one of the first phrases I hear is, 'okay, so now I need to raise the finance'. Everyone seems to labour under the illusion that you need lots of money to start a business and that there is money out there for the taking, once you become an entrepreneur.

Well, there is good news and bad news.

The good news is that there is indeed millions of pounds or dollars sloshing around 'out there' for investment in new or existing businesses. And why shouldn't you have some of it? Investors – and that includes the big pension and insurance companies – need their money to be working for them and they are always looking for great ideas to invest in. I was heart–warmed to read the story, 'Anyone Can Do It' written by the brother and sister pair Sahar and Bobby Hashemi, founders of Coffee Republic, who managed to borrow £100,000 from a bank to start Coffee Republic's first shop in South Molton Street, London. It wasn't easy, they were rejected by about 26 banks before they found the *one* that said 'yes'. But they raised the money and the rest is history.

The bad news is that banks only lend about 50% of any monies needed (and always want security such as your house or Government Loan Guarantee scheme), virtually no–one wants to lend or invest money to a startup and no–one wants to lend or invest money to pay you a salary and that is what most people mean when they say 'raise finance' to start their business. Bobby Hashemi had worked in investment banking but he commented that it was much easier to raise millions of pounds for clients than it was to raise a paltry £100,000. And their business plan did not include salaries for the founders for the first year at least – they never did say what they lived on! They struggled with conventional lenders because banks like security and they didn't have any. They eventually found out about the Government Small Loans Guarantee Scheme which guarantees up to 70–80% of lending where there is no security.

Did you know that there are Business Angels? These are private investors, very wealthy and successful individuals, often retired business people, who will lend money and give their time to the businesses they invest in. Giving these fledgling business owners the benefit of their wisdom, experience and contacts. This sounds great, doesn't it? They are contacted via the National Association of Business Angels in the UK, or NBAN (*www.nban.co.uk*).

I went down that whole road with my ArtistManager.com concept and also paid a large sum to be (unsuccessfully) featured in the Venture Capital Report (www.vcr1978.com). Ironically we were featured in the same issue as Sahar and Bobby Hashemi, who successfully went on to raise the £2 million expansion money they were looking for, to open their next six shops.

But before you go rushing off to visit those websites, consider this. This is the part that not even my very excellent accountants thought to mention, presumably assuming that I knew such an essential piece of obvious business information already. Business Angels will be looking for a clear exit strategy within three to five years maximum and a minimum return on their investment of 30–35% per annum.

What does this mean exactly?

Essentially, Business Angels want to see how they will be able to get their money back out, within a reasonable time frame. They will want to keep a share in the company in return for 'lending' you the use of their money, but they want that money back quite soon to invest in another opportunity.

They also want to increase their money (or get a 'return on investment') by 30–35% per annum (that's *per annum*) or they don't even get out of bed to get their cheque books.

So for every £100 invested in your company, they will want £135 back in year one, £182 back in year two, £246 back in year three, £332 back in year four and £448 back in year five. They won't necessarily expect it to be paid in years one to four, but in year five they will look at their £100 and expect £1343 back in total.

Plus the shares they still own which they will expect to pay a dividend based on profits.

Until I started reading business and wealth creation books, my business plans barely knew what an exit strategy was, let alone a return on investment! And I thought you shouldn't show a profit in your first three years of trading because it was better for tax purposes. No wonder I never raised any finance!

This is the really nitty–gritty question. If a professional investor or a high street bank wouldn't want to invest in or lend to your business, why would you even consider it?

After all, you have a lot more to lose if it all goes wrong. Why would you want to put your time (very expensive) and money (very risky) into a business that no–one else would touch with a barge pole? Don't we think that perhaps they may know what they are talking about?

Luckily for the state of the economy in both the UK and the US, entrepreneurs (or technicians having an entrepreneurial seizure) always think they know better than banks and investors, so they carry on regardless and about 2% of them succeed. Those 2% go on to create great wealth, create jobs for many others and give a much needed boost to the economy. Wouldn't it be good though, to start with the end in mind and set our new business up right first time? The end being success, freedom, wealth, security, an exit strategy, a profitable business and one that doesn't depend on us working in it, to succeed.

Perhaps the best book I have ever read on how to set up a business so that a third party will want to invest in, or even buy your business one day, is 'Rich Dad's Guide To Investment' by Robert Kiyosaki. A bit of a dull title but a great book! The first two thirds of the book are about the different levels of investing, and the differing levels of sophistication of investors. The most sophisticated of all are the Business Angels, who invest directly into start up operations, either small concerns or the companies that are going straight to the stock market in the form of IPO's (Initial Public Offerings). High risk and massively high return investments.

The important part of the book for the purposes of this module though, is the final third. It tells the sophisticated investor step–by–step what to look for in a great company to invest in. And remember, as you will be investing time and money into your own business, this is the blueprint for setting up your own business so that it's worth you investing in.

ACTION STEP

What is your ROI?

If you already have a business, think about the startup costs and how much time you spent setting it up. Are you getting a 35% return on your investment, year on year? Will you get a 35% return on your investment in ten years even? What is your exit strategy? Are you going to work in your business till you drop, or will you eventually sell it? Would anyone invest in your business right now? Would you? Would it sell today and if not, why not? Would you buy it? If not, why not? These could be some of the most important questions you ever ask yourself about your business.

You can use the ROI model used in the property module and adapt it for using to evaluate business opportunities. In fact, you can use it to compare any opportunity – like with like.

If you are thinking of setting up a new business, think about the projected return on your investment and what your exit strategy will be – how will you get your money out again? Most entrepreneurs think that they have to sink everything into their business in terms of time and money; this shows commitment after all. A serious businessperson, however, would be planning to get their money out again as soon as possible, with a good ROI, while leaving the business to thrive healthily and continue to pay them dividends based on profits.

Buy 'E–Myth Revisited' and 'Rich Dad's Guide to Investment' and devour them. Make notes, underline, and take on board their wisdom.

Your business will never be the same.

Predictable Miracles

In his great book on leadership called 'Synchronicity – The Inner Path of Leadership' Joseph Jaworsky talks about the incredible phenomenon of 'predictable miracles'.

How the universe conspires to help you open doors and send the right people your way, as soon as you have made up your mind to take action to improve things for yourself or your business. And how amazing things start to happen. Things that, if you told someone about them afterward, would seem incredible or far-fetched.

It's a great book, inspirational, touching and down to earth; one that all entrepreneurs should read. Chris Barrow recommended it and I took it on holiday. Then my sister Sarah arrived and she read it too – we have had some great conversations about the predicable miracles that have occurred so far in our lives.

Just for the record, in the same way that I read but never took action on the 'how to' books, and in the same way that my natural cynicism stopped me reading 'personal development' books for years, I took a while to come around to reading 'leadership' type books because I had an assumption that leadership books were for people who work in big organisations and have to lead/manage lots of other people.

Then I realised that to be a great entrepreneur you have to be able to lead teams of people who are perhaps all self employed, and that could be even harder. They need to buy into your vision even more than employees do because they have the choice to walk away.

But most of all you have to be able to lead yourself!

Joseph Jaworsky says that two critical ingredients are needed for 'predicable miracles' to take place. The first is that you have a vision – a big vision, a sexy vision, an inspirational vision – without necessarily knowing how you are going to achieve it.

The second is that you become committed to that vision, which you can only do by beginning to take action. And the more action you take, the more committed you will become. Then the Universe starts to work with you and you become part of what great physicists like Dr David Bohm, Professor of Theoretical Physics at London's Birkbeck College, call the 'unfolding of the universe' and that is when 'predictable miracles' start to occur. Yep, something *that* esoteric has actually got a basis in science and physics – isn't that fascinating?

Jaworsky describes the moment of commitment, of starting to take action, as a kind of tipping over, 'not so much a decision about what I ought to do – rather, I could not do otherwise... it was at this moment that my words became action'.

When you have a business idea, if you start to do some research, without necessarily saying to yourself that you are going to take action yet, there will come a time (if it's the right idea for you) when you will tip over into taking action, into becoming committed. And the more action you take, the more committed you will become. Until it becomes unthinkable that you would ever *not* have taken action.

I seem to attract a lot of professional people as clients; people like dentists, doctors and lawyers. They are highly intelligent and organised. However, they are often victim of analysis paralysis – where they spend so much time thinking about and analysing something, wanting it to be perfect before they start, that they never get started. I always tell my clients that it is better to take action, any action, even possibly the wrong action, because something will happen, something will start to occur.

They will not be in the same place as they were and the very act of taking action will start things moving out there, out in the universe, where they can't even be seen yet. The 'biggest' of them will often trust me (even though they may secretly think I'm talking mystical mumbo jumbo) and do something, *anything*. Then they are often amazed at the results!

ACTION STEP

What could you take action on?

Can you think about an idea for a business you have had in the past that you never took any action on? Take that idea down, just for a moment, dust it off and let's use it as an example. Pick something big, something exciting, something out of the safe ole' playground and well into the adventure ground (as Jack Black of Mindstore would say). Don't worry about it being the 'right' business, the 'perfect' business, the 'ultimate' business. Just pick one.

What one action could you take, to see if that business is of interest to you or even a viable option for someone else? Could you make a call, look up something on the internet, get a reference book down? What one thing would move that idea forward by just a tiny amount?

There is a great tool invented by Mark Forster, Time Management Coach, called 'I'll just get the file out'. He uses it when he or a client is avoiding doing something they know they should do, or something they want to do but just can't get around to. Now you know that starting a business on the side of your day job is something that you need to do, for the good of your wealth creation activities. But you just keep putting it off? So why not set aside a time every day, or every week, to 'just get the file out' on your business idea. You don't have to open it, but just sit for a moment and think about the one tiny action you could take to move things forward just a tiny bit.

The Entrepreneurial Traps

So what are the Entrepreneurial Traps?

Jaworsky talks about a book called, 'The Hero With A Thousand Faces' by Joseph Campbell, where Campbell talks about the heroic quest or journey, describing the changes that people and organisations alike can go through. The picture begins with the 'wasteland', the inauthentic life where nothing feels good, everything feels empty; before you receive the 'call to adventure', to become what we are meant to become, to achieve our 'vital design'. It may take years and we may ignore it for a long time, but if we hear and respond to the call we cross the threshold and begin the journey, into the unknown. This is when the 'predicable miracles' start to occur, like unseen helping hands. This is the point at which our freedom and destiny merge, where we encounter a series of traps, trials, tests and ordeals.

These traps, trials, tests and ordeals test our commitment to the direction we have taken and they provide opportunities to learn from failure. This is probably the most useful part of the journey as it teaches us different ways to think. Remember in 'Conversations With Millionaires' where they say that the best reason to decide to become a millionaire is because of what you will learn along the way?

The traps along the way can cause you to regress to your old ways of thinking and acting. They hinder the process of your becoming part of the unfolding of the universe and its abundance. We often fall into those traps when the stakes are really high, when lots is happening, when things are going beautifully and a lot of money is involved.

When we fall into a trap, Jaworsky says, a vicious circle can begin to operate and things go from bad to worse very quickly. But if we are aware of our traps and remain alert to their danger, we can largely avoid their consequences.

The Trap of Responsibility...

is where you get cold feet because you feel that you are indispensable to the whole process, responsible for all the people involved, everyone is depending on you. The focus is on you instead of the larger calling. This is where you start to overwork, as an entrepreneur you become too hands-on, feel overwhelmed, overworked, stressed and the load starts to feel unbearable. Your productivity and effectiveness goes down the drain and instead of experiencing an effortless flow, you scramble to fight fires all the time.

You can get out of this trap by seeing things the way they really are, namely that there is nothing special about you particularly that allows you to operate in the flow of the universe; it's a way of operating that is available to everyone. You have to learn to make space for the creativity to come through, and while you can feel 'concern' for and 'care' about your employees and colleagues, you shouldn't feel responsible for them. You shouldn't 'worry' about them. This trap is simply a habit of thought and we when we can recognise it, it loses its power and it just melts away.

The Trap of Dependency...

is where we feel so dependent on key staff, key colleagues or the details of a key plan, that we feel our enterprise will flounder without them. This feeling makes us compromise the stand we would normally take for the dream. We stop being straightforward with people for fear of offending or fear they will leave the team and we pussyfoot around instead of speaking from our centre. We forget that it was the flow and the call from the centre that attracted them in the first place. This trap comes from our fear of inadequacy and unworthiness. This trap can also lead you to think of a change of direction as weakness, as a need to adapt to changing circumstances as a lack of commitment to the Plan, forgetting that plans can change as people and circumstances change.

You end up focused on the process rather than the end result you are trying to create. And the result is not about what you are trying to achieve for yourself, but about the result you want to achieve 'for its own sake' as Jaworsky puts it. He quotes Robert Frost as saying 'All great things are done for their own sake' and I've written in the margin 'just for fun'.

My eight year old daughter thought that I wrote that to indicate that I was writing in a book just for fun but I was actually remembering that some of the most amazing things in my life have happened because I thought they would 'be a laugh'. Once you focus on doing something for its own sake that door opens, hidden hands help, incredible co–incidences occur and things move faster than you ever dreamed they would.

The Trap of Overactivity...

is not where, in the beginning, you are getting loads done, creativity is rolling, everything is working in the flow, it's all just happening. It comes later when there are a myriad of tiny decisions to be made, details to be juggled, and your sense of true freedom and clarity gets overwhelmed in the day to day minutiae. This is where you are so busy deciding which colour the tiles in the staff loos should be, that you haven't got time to take a call and you miss a phone call from your potentially biggest client ever. This is where it becomes really easy to blame other people for the situation but it's really all about us, our history and our feelings of unworthiness.

The Traps of Responsibility and Dependency get a lot of their energy from a fear of no alternative yet there is *always* an alternative. It's just that we are unable to see or unwilling to look. Once you are willing to accept that there is an alternative you can look at the traps more objectively, 'there I go again, thinking I'm indispensable!' or, 'look at me, overly depending on Bert and thinking that if he leaves we are sunk!' or, 'how funny, that part of the plan obviously won't achieve the end result now, we had better change it'.

The Trap of Overactivity can be overcome easily by doing less and making time to think. We need an anchor, the reminder of why we are there in the first place, of what is important. Getting together with the core team gives everyone a chance to maintain a space at the heart of all of the activity, so that everyone can be re–nurtured together by the things still wanting to happen, the unfolding still to come. The discipline of reconnecting with each other, with having meaningful dialogue, is so important – especially when it feels like there is no time for another meeting!

Jaworsky gives us the good news, that it's really easy to get back in the flow, once you realise. And I would add that the way to tell that we are out of the flow, is when it all just seems like hard work. We have been brought up to think that in order to succeed, we must work hard. Not so. In order to succeed, you must be in the flow.

ACTION STEP

Which Trap Are You Falling Into Right Now?

If I were talking to a businessperson and I had to take a bet which of the traps they were falling into, my answer would depend on the stage they were at with their business.

If they were in the startup phase I would say The Trap of Dependency because they would be finding lots of skills, equipment, finance or people that they felt they needed, before they could start.

If they were more established, I would be that they were falling into the Trap of Overactivity, because they would be working long hours, feeling that their business would die if they are not there 24/7 and unable to take the time to plan, unable to see the woods for the trees.

And the more established the business is, the more the danger of the Trap of Responsibility. I am particularly prone to this one, having been the eldest of four children, being responsible for others was drummed into me at a very early age. It even manifests itself in my choice of tavernas while on holiday, because I am so friendly with Llias at Pefko Taverna, I feel that my choice of where to eat impacts on his business and that I am responsible for that!

Take a good look at yourself, note which trap you fall into most regularly, and pin up a note where you can see it, every day. Remind yourself that success shouldn't be hard work, if it is, then you have fallen into a trap. Take some time, and get back in the flow.

Intention -v- Attention

One day, early in my coaching career, I panicked about not having enough clients. I scheduled a call to my first ever coach, Rachel Turner, to discuss emergency measures I could take. However, before the call, I heard Rachel's voice in my head (sign of a good coach, note!) asking me, 'well, Nicola, just what *have* you done to attract clients?'

And I thought to myself, well, we discussed this, this and that, and I *could* have done this, this and that. But at the end of the day, what *have* I actually done? Not much at all, was the truthful answer.

It is almost as though we don't take action because we have already convinced ourselves that it won't work. And this moment of insight was all it required for me to think, 'well, I don't want to tell her these things don't work, because I haven't actually tried any of them'. Is it an inbuilt cynicism, a bit like the cynicism that stopped me ever reading personal development or wealth creation books in the past?

So the coaching call was a bit redundant in the end, because it was all about me reporting in to Rachel on the actions taken since the day before (some of which were already working) rather than me moaning on to my coach about all the things I hadn't done, which weren't working.

Interesting huh? Whenever I speak to my clients and they are complaining that they haven't got enough clients, I always ask them what they are actually doing, on a regular basis, to attract clients. Not what they think they are doing, or what they think they could do, or what they have heard works, or does not work. But what they are actually doing day by day, week by week. I also ask what has worked in the past, what they used to do that they are not doing now.

Not much is usually the answer, and certainly not enough of the things that actually work!

Then, when reading Michael Gerber's 'E–Myth Revisited' I came across the phrase, 'having the intention but not paying enough attention' and it leapt off the page at me as a neat way to describe the above phenomena.

Entrepreneurs are particularly prone to this – ask any entrepreneur or business person what One Thing could they do, or change in their business, that would make a huge difference to their business and they will usually know the answer. Ask them why they are not doing it, and they will say something, anything, to explain why they 'have the intention' but are just not 'paying it the attention'. It is as if they know what the one thing is, but don't really believe that it will work. Or if they do, that they are not ready for the consequences if it does work. Mark Forster, Time Management Guru & Coach, calls this the Anti-Goal and tells us how to deal with it most effectively. Find Mark at www.markforster.net

Another manifestation of this idea is when you do anything and everything, every day except the most important (income generating or people oriented) thing. You usually will do what is most urgent, what shouts loudest from your in–tray or to–do list, rather than the one thing that would make the most difference in your business life.

A great way to remind yourself of how important this concept is, would be to put the phrase, 'when I have the intention, I pay the attention' on your screensaver and then write, 'what is most important here? What is just urgent?' at the beginning of every day in your diary, put it in your outlook or palm pilot, or just pin it up above your desk.

This is not about time management or prioritising. It is about thinking like a leader. About rising above the norm to be pro–active rather than reactive. You can do it, you know. Because it *is* important.

ACTION STEP

What one thing would make a major difference to your business right now? What one thing do you have the intention of getting around to, but you constantly avoid paying the attention to?

What one thing on your to–do list is the most important rather than just urgent busy–ness?

Why not do that first?

Going Forward

Being a business person is often looked down on by creative people. I spent years in the fashion and music industries and the creative types looked down on the 'suits' and felt sorry for them. But, contrary to popular belief, I have grown to realise that being a business person and working on something that you are passionate about, is fun and very, very creative.

Chasing the money was also looked down upon with people who aspire to be financially successful being perceived as somehow flawed, grasping and cut–throat. We know differently now, don't we? Having enough money can set you free.

You now know that you can create a business out of any passion, hobby, interest or life experience. The trick is to create a business, not a job. Don't spoil it for yourself by setting yourself up to fail rather than succeed and have fun doing it.

So what would I say are the essential building blocks of starting your own business?

Try new ideas out, research them and see if you are moved to take just a little bit more action. See if you are tempted to become committed.

Read the books I recommend, the 'E–Myth Revisited' by Michael E Gerber, 'Rich Dad's Guide To Investment' by Robert Kiyosaki, 'Synchronicity' by Joseph Jaworski and 'Anyone Can Do It' by Sahar and Bobby Hashemi. Best of all, make sure you read 'Ready Fire Aim' by Michael Masterson.

Look at your personality type, Entrepreneur, Manager or Technician, and assemble a team that includes the missing links for you. Find someone who has succeeded in what you want to do and ignore all the folks who offer advice so freely but who haven't succeeded in what you want to do. Cheap advice can be the most expensive advice of all.

Don't despair if you already have a business that isn't quite working. As Sahar Hashemi says, just a 1% change every day brings about a 100% change in just three.

Concentrate every day on what is important rather than what just feels urgent. Have the intention and then pay the attention.

If you are working, start a 'freedom fund' and start your business alongside your day job. If your business is exciting enough to spend the next year or two of your life on, it's exciting enough to miss a bit of TV now for.

And if all else fails to get you moving, think about the tax breaks!

ACTION STEP

Check out your local Business Link or Enterprise Centre for low cost or free training on all aspects of running a business – you can often get a free business evaluation session.

THE MONEY GYM WORKOUT PLAN

These are the actions I will take in the next month, arising from Module 9: Mind Your Own Business

1. _____

2. _____

3. _____

4. _____

5. _____

6. _____

7. _____

8. _____

9. _____

10. _____

11. _____

12. _____

13. _____

14. _____

15. _____

16. _____

17. _____

18. _____

19. _____

20. _____

Signed: _____ Date: _____

Summary

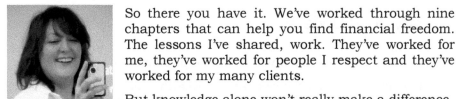

So there you have it. We've worked through nine chapters that can help you find financial freedom. The lessons I've shared, work. They've worked for me, they've worked for people I respect and they've worked for my many clients.

But knowledge alone won't really make a difference.

It's up to you to apply what you've learned and start making your money work harder for you. You now have the knowledge so you have no excuse not to put it into practice.

Now don't just leave this book on the shelf like all the others you've read and forget about it. Do something now – today – to make your financial dreams closer.

I wish you luck and look forward to hearing how you get on!

Best Wishes

Nicola Cairncross
www.TheMoneyGym.com
www.NicolaCairncross.com

Take Things Further...

January 2010 Update

If you enjoyed this book you may be interested to know that I'm working on my second book which will be published in mid 2010.

Drawing on my experiences as a wealth coach, entrepreneur, professional speaker and internet marketer, it's all about success and why some people find it so hard to take action and create success in their lives (and what to do about it!)

Inspired and illustrated by the stories of the many thousands of people I've seen at seminars and workshops and the many hundreds of Money Gym clients that have passed through our workshops in the last six odd years.

And also inspired by the many mega successful people I've been lucky enough to meet and interview for the book.

If you would like to get on the VIP Priority Notification List for my next book (along with any free gifts on offer!) visit me here and add your Name and Primary email into the box: *www.nicolacairncross.com/blog/books*

The Money Gym – 30 Day Free Trial: Silver Membership

To access all of the tools and great stuff mentioned in this book, along with a monthly wealth creation webinar and regularly updated list of useful links, just follow these simple instructions.

Visit *www.themoneygym.com* and put your name and email address in the 'Wealth Tips' box.

You should then look out for an email that you need to click into to confirm your interest.

You will then receive email confirmation from TheMoneyGym.com that you are subscribed to our mailing list and information on how to access your free 30 day trial.

Speaking

Would You Like Nicola To Speak At Your Event On Wealth Creation Or Internet Marketing?

Nicola loves to speak on her core topics of wealth creation, property investing, internet marketing and success and entrepreneurialism.

Just email *Nicola@NicolaCairncross.com*

Mentoring

Would You Like Nicola & Her Team To Mentor You On Making Money Online?

Nicola has created an affordable two-level mentoring programme called 'Hidden Star To Superstar' to enable people with a real world business to harness the power of the internet OR people with a passion, hobby, skill or knowledge to make money from what they love.

Just visit *www.NicolaCairncross.com/blog* to find out more.

Recommended Resources

I have personally read all of the following books and highly recommend them all. They are listed in my recommended reading order, but you may choose. You may also choose to listen, rather than read, if that's how you learn best!

Some of the books are US based, some UK based, but all have information worth acquiring for anyone serious about wealth creation, wherever you may live. The numbers after the names are the ISBN numbers to help you find them.

Practical Finances & Wealth Creation

Swimming with Piranha Makes You Hungry, Colin Turner 190495605X

Rich Dad, Poor Dad, Robert Kiyosaki 044656740X

One Minute Millionaire, Mark Victor Hanson & Robert Allen 0307451569

Richest Man In Babylon, George S Clason 0451205367

Debt Proof Living, Mary Hunt 0976079119

Think Yourself Rich, Sharon Maxwell Magnus 0735202230

Wildly Wealthy Fast, Sandy Forster 1600373453

The Millionaire Mind, Thomas J Stanley 0740718584

Mind Of A Millionaire, T.Harv Eker 0060763280

The Wealth Workout, Marcus De Maria 1905823509

The More Metaphysical Side of Wealth Creation

Science of Getting Rich, Wallace T Wattles 1442169176

You Were Born Rich, Bob Proctor 0965626431

Think & Grow Rich, Napoleon Hill 1449911331

The Dynamic Laws of Prosperity, Catherine Ponder 1604598646

Anything by the marvellous Joe Vitale – love all his books! Perhaps start with The Attractor Factor 0470286423

Property Investing

Property Made Simple, Peter Stanley 1905430167

Building Wealth: From Rags to Riches Through Real Estate, Russ Whitney 0684800519

Nothing Down For the 2000's Robert Allen 0743261550

Rich Dad's Advisors: The ABC's Of Real Estate, Dolf De Roos 0446691844

Buy To Let: The Keystep Series, Stuart Powers (UK Based) 0953756327

The Buy To Let Bible, Ajay Ahuja (UK Based) 1905261705

Your Money For Nothing & Your Property For Free, Andy Shaw (not available on Amazon but here's Andy's website *www.AndyShaw.com*

Minding Your Own Business

E–Myth Revisited, Michael Gerber 0887307280

Rich Dad's Guide To Investing, Robert Kiyosaki 0446677469

E–Myth Manager, Michael Gerber 0887309593

Ready Fire Aim (Zero to £100 Million In No Time Flat, Michael Masterson 0470182024

Get Clients Now!, CJ Hayden 0814473741

One Minute Manager, Jack Canfield 0688014291

Anyone Can Do It: Building Coffee Republic From Our Kitchen Table: 57 Real–life laws on entrepreneurship, Sahar Hashemi, Bobby Hashemi 1841127655

The Gorillas Want Bananas, Joe Gregory & Debbie Jenkins 0954568109, *www.leanmarketing.co.uk*

Profit From Your Passion - The Internet

StrikingItRich.com, Jaclyn Easton 007018724X

Multiple Streams of Internet Income: How ordinary people make extraordinary money online, Robert Allen 0471714550

The Wealth Author, Joe Gregory & Debbie Jenkins 1905430698

Equity Investing

Rich Dad's Guide To Investing, Robert Kiyosaki 0446677469

The Armchair Investor, Bernice Cohen 0752811738

The Zulu Principle, Jim Slater 1905641915

Prophecy, Robert Kiyosaki 0446690341

Personal Development & Leadership

7 Habits of Highly Effective People, Stephen Covey 0743269519

Who Moved My Cheese, Jack Canfield   0399144463

Synchronicity: The Inner Path of Leadership, Joseph Jaworski 1576750310

MindStore, Jack Black 0954715543

Get Everything Done & Still Have Time to Play, Mark Forster 0340746203

The Road Less Travelled, M. Scott Peck 0684847248

Conversations With God, Neale Donald Walsh 0399142789

Outliers, Malcolm Gladwell 0316017922

Predictably Irrational, Dan Ariely 006135323X

Bibliography

1001 Ways to Market Your Books, John Kremer, 091241149X

The 22 Immutable Laws of Marketing, Al Ries & Jack Trout, 1861976100

The 4-Hour Workweek, Timothy Ferris, 0091923727

Aiming At Amazon, Aaron Shepard, 093849743X

The Amazon Bestseller Plan, Debbie Jenkins & Joe Gregory, www.publishingacademy.com

The Art of Contrary Thinking, Humphrey Neill, 087004110X

Bare Knuckle Negotiating, Simon Hazeldine, 1905430140

Bare Knuckle Selling, Simon Hazeldine, 1905430051

Blocks, Tom Evans, *www.publishingacademy.com*

The Chicago Manual of Style, University of Chicago Press, 0226104036

Dan Poynter's Self-Publishing Manual: How to Write, Print and Sell Your Own Book, Dan Poynter, 1568601425

E-myth Revisited, Michael E Gerber, 0887307280

Get Your Book Published, Suzan St Maur

Go it Alone: The Streetwise Secrets of Self-employment, Geoff Burch, 1841124702

Google Adwords for Dummies, Howie Jacobson, 0470455772

The Gorillas Want Bananas, Joe Gregory & Debbie Jenkins, 0954568109

How to Get Rich, Felix Denis, 009192166X

Influence, Robert Cialdini, 006124189X

It's Called Work for a Reason! Your Success Is Your Own Damn Fault, Larry Winget, 159240281X

Kickstart Your Business, Robert Craven, 0753509733

MediaMasters, Alan Stevens & Jeremy Nicholas, 1905430612

The Midas Method, Stuart G Goldsmith, 1871379008

The Mindmap Book, Tony Buzan & Barry Buzan, 1406612790

The Money Gym, Nicola Cairncross, 0954568184

No B.S. Direct Marketing, Dan Kennedy, 1932531572

No B.S. Wealth Attraction for Entrepreneurs, 193253167X

Oxford Guide To Style, Robert Ritter, 0198691750

Permission Marketing, Seth Godin, 1416526668

Persuasion Skills Black Book, Rintu Basu, 190543054X

Powerwriting, Suzan St Maur, 0273659065

Print On Demand Book Publishing, Morris Rosenthal, 0972380132

ProBlogger: Blogging Your Way to a 6 Figure Income, Darren Rowse & Chris Garrett, 0470246677

Release The Book Within, Jo Parfitt, 1905430264

Selling The Invisible: A Field Guide to Modern Marketing, Harry Beckwith, 0446520942

Strategies of Genius, Volume 1, Robert Dilts, 091699032X

Trance-formations: NLP and the Structure of Hypnosis, John Grinder & Richard Bandler, 0911226230

Tribes, Seth Godin, 0749939753

Unleashing the Ideavirus, Seth Godin, 074322065X

The Well-Fed Self-Publisher, Peter Bowerman, 0967059860

The Writers' and Artists' Yearbook 2010, 1408111276

STONE
SOUP

THE SECRET RECIPE FOR
MAKING SOMETHING
FROM NOTHING

MYTHICAL STORYTELLING
REMINISCENT OF
PAULO COELHO
Tom Evans, Author of Blocks,
www.thebookwright.com

Including
Bill Liao's
$25,000
Investment
Challenge

BILL LIAO
CO-FOUNDER OF XING

www.bookshaker.com

mum
ultrapreneur

"Filled to breaking with
the insights of over thirty
incredible business mums"
Saira Khan Director of Miamoo,
author of 'PUSH for Success' and
Star of TV's The Apprentice

discover the 8 essential secrets
to starting, running and building a
successful mum–based business

susan ödev and mark weeks

www.bookshaker.com

SECRETS

OF SUCCESSFUL
WOMEN
ENTREPRENEURS

HOW TEN LEADING BUSINESS WOMEN
TURNED A GOOD IDEA INTO A FORTUNE

linda bennett glenda stone geetie singh penny streeter josephine carpenter

michelle mone yvonne thompson helen swaby marilyn orcharton julie meyer

SUE STOCKDALE

www.bookshaker.com

The Wealthy Author

The Fast Profit Method For
Writing, Publishing & Selling
Your Non-Fiction Book

JOE GREGORY
DEBBIE JENKINS

www.bookshaker.com